Equality in action:
a way forward with Persona Dolls

Equality in action:
a way forward with Persona Dolls

Babette Brown

tb

Trentham Books

Stoke on Trent, UK and Sterling, USA

Trentham Books Limited
Westview House   22883 Quicksilver Drive
734 London Road   Sterling
Oakhill   VA 20166-2012
Stoke on Trent   USA
Staffordshire
England ST4 5NP

First published 2008

British Library Cataloguing-in-Publication Data
A catalogue record for this book is available from the British Library

ISBN: 978 1 85856 435 7

Cover photograph: Natasha Brown

Designed and typeset by Trentham Print Design Ltd, Chester and
printed in Great Britain by Cromwell Press Ltd, Trowbridge.

Contents

Acknowledgements

Warm thanks to Sue Adler, Cathy Brown, Jenny Brown, Peter Brown, Eve Cook, Liz de Keller, Sally Elton-Chalcraft, Sue Ford, Gillian Klein, Emma Kosmin, Elaine McClement, Ruth Moran, Deborah Scaife, Carol Smith, Tracy Smith and Charlotte Tagart for their contributions, support and thoughtful advice.

Thanks also to Leon Fletcher-Tomenius, Vicky Hutchin, Glenda MacNaughton and Helen Penn for their instructive and constructive comments on the methodology of the evaluation project and to Holly Kosmin for analysing the data.

To everyone who gave up their valuable time to complete our questionnaire and who agreed to be interviewed, many thanks – without your input the project would not have got off the ground.

Cover photo: Natasha Brown

Dedication

*To our trainers whose commitment, skill and hard work are making a
difference to the lives of children and their families all over the UK:
Jane Louth; Jane Slater; Marie Spencer; Meredith Wilson;
Meryl Shepherd; Ruth Moran; Sue Sheppy and to
Meeta Johnson our training administrator.*

Introduction

Cowardice asks the question, 'Is it safe?' Expediency asks the question, 'Is it politic?' Vanity asks the question, 'Is it popular?' But, conscience asks the question, 'Is it right?' And there comes a time when one must take a position that is neither safe, nor politic, nor popular, but one must take it because one's conscience tells one that it is right.

In the end, we will remember not the words of our enemies, but the silence of our friends.

Inspiring words from Martin Luther King Junior. *Remaining Awake Through a Great Revolution*, Washington (31 March 1968)

Enabling children to share their ideas and experiences is something that educators do all the time. However, not everyone creates an environment that encourages children to express what they honestly feel about how they are treated and the way they treat others. Ann Longfield, chief executive of 4Children writing in *Nursery World* (28/6/07:30) suggests that:

> Involving children and young people is no longer an optional extra. National developments such as *Every Child Matters* and the Children Act, set in the context of international policy like the UN Convention on the Rights of the Child, mean that we have to talk with them and listen to them. Work from the DfES from *Exploring the Field of Listening and Consulting with Young Children* (2003) indicates that even very young children develop higher self-esteem and better social skills as a result of being listened to ... The benefits of involvement have led to calls by the House of Commons Education and Skills Committee for the Government to back a statutory basis for school councils. ... Participation is a child's right and it shows them the respect they deserve. It also connects children to those responsible for their care and improves service delivery. We all need to see the world through the eyes of the child.

Conversation, open ended questions and thinking out loud all encourage children's critical thinking, listening and reflective skills. Two major research projects, (EPPE) Effective Provision of Pre-school Education (2004) and (REPEY) Researching Effective Pedagogy in the Early Years (2002) propose that one way to identify high-quality practice is to assess the extent to which children are helped to develop their thinking skills.

According to Marion Dowling, writing in *Nursery World* (February 2008:19)

> The interim findings of the Primary Review revealed through interviews with children that some as young as four years think deeply about issues in the world that confront us all. They try to make sense about the worrying turmoil in their family lives, the effects of climate change, crime, violence and the tragedy of wars that they witness daily in the media. ... Practitioners increasingly recognise the need to be alert to children's views and ideas and to consider the conditions that help them to grow and share their thinking.

In the following example, cited by MacNaughton and Williams (1998) Maria, a child care worker in an upper-class suburb in Melbourne, used a current issue to spark a discussion with a group of 4 and 5 year old children who would soon be going to school. She showed them a photo of a crowded refugee camp.

> Maria: Has anyone seen pictures like this on TV or in the newspaper? What questions do you have about these people?
>
> The children's questions were:
>
> - who are these people?
> - what are they doing there?
> - why are there so many of them?
> - how did they get there?
> - where do they eat?
> - where do they sleep?
> - are they families?
>
> Maria encouraged the children to reflect on their questions and to make connections between them. She then began exploring some answers with them such as what do you think they're doing there? And where might the food come from?

She listened carefully to the children's suggestions, taking care to show them that she valued all their answers. At the end of the session Maria fed back their initial questions and they all discussed how much they had found out about the refugees. She praised the children for being so curious and for sticking to the topic at hand.

Powerful Dolls

Developing children's capacity to think critically is a skill that the Persona Doll approach sets out to promote. During the storytelling sessions educators act as facilitators, stepping back to give children space to identify the Doll's feelings, to think, reflect, discuss their ideas and problem solve. Given this opportunity, children are able to talk about how they are treated and the way they treat others. In the process their knowledge base, their horizons and their emotional intelligence and literacy skills are boosted. This is how an educator being interviewed for the 'Evaluating anti-discriminatory practice project' (see chapter 8) described the impact of a Doll:

> I remember a girl who had quite a lot of problems with behaviour and getting on with other children – so I brought in the Doll who was having similar problems and she just fell in love with him. She said after a while that she had never had so much in common with anyone in her whole life.

Educators ensure that they present issues sensitively and that they listen to the children's ideas actively, supportively and respectfully. Because the Persona Doll approach is non-threatening, they develop the confidence to raise controversial social issues. J Silin (2002) a visiting scholar at the Centre for Equity and Innovation in Early Childhood in Melbourne believes that children benefit from discussing these issues:

> My years of helping teachers to talk about difficult social issues such as HIV/AIDS, substance abuse, and community violence have taught me that young children often respond to such issues long after the formal, adult-led discussions about them have ended. Their responses often appear in play and with concrete materials, undoubtedly mediated by individual personalities and life circumstances. ... I believe, however, that it is the educator's responsibility to explore with students how society is responding to these difficult events – from managing the physical destruction at ground zero to pursuing the war in Afghanistan. And, yes, this may mean encountering difficult emotions and unanswerable questions in the class. We will be so much the wiser for acknowledging our ignorance, serving as models in our search for understanding and in our willingness to listen to the children.

Children at the foundation stage and at key stages 1 and 2 have the facility to be fully involved in pretend stories and situations. They appreciate that Persona Dolls are Dolls which have their own individual personalities, names, ages, gender, culture, language(s) and religion or no religion. Boys and girls are keen to know where the Dolls live and sleep; who lives with them; their favourite foods, games, sports and TV programmes, as well as the ones they dislike; the things they enjoy doing and the things they can't do because they're too young or perhaps have a disability.

Educators working with older children may think that their class, especially if it includes macho boys, would be scathing but in fact in settings/schools around Britain as well as in Germany, Iceland, Hungary and South Africa, boys are responding with compassion and empathy to the Dolls and their stories.

This report came from an educational psychologist working in Johannesburg, South Africa. Staff had been alerted to the fact that three of the children had lost primary caregivers. A boy's mother, a girl's grandmother and another girl's step-mother had all died. The teacher felt overwhelmed and anxious about talking to the children so the educational psychologist ran two Persona Doll sessions:

> During the first session the Doll, Ketiwe, was introduced to the children. They were told that her father had passed away during the holidays and that she was very sad and was missing him. She was also feeling scared coming to talk to them about something that was so sad – she had stood outside the room for a long time before coming in. All the children except S, the boy whose mother had died, spoke to her. They told her that they were sorry she was sad, that they loved her and that they would buy her presents to make her happy. Ketiwe 'told' them that she was sad and that it was ok for her to be sad for a while.

> In the second session, Ketiwe reminded the children about why she had come to speak to them. M started off by telling Ketiwe that her granny had passed away on her farm. Then each child told of a loved one who had died. Remarkably, S, who had been very quiet and not spoken before about his mother dying stood up and told Ketiwe and the class. There were shocked gasps from some of the other children. When they had all had their turn (it seemed that one or two made up their stories in order to be able to

contribute)they went off to blow their noses and to go to the toilet. After a few minutes, only three children were left in the circle. When they all returned, Ketiwe 'reflected' on how very difficult it was to talk about people that you love who have died. She suggested that maybe that was why some children needed to go away for a few minutes and that it was ok if they needed a break. She thanked them for sharing their stories with her and that even though it made her sad it made her feel a little bit better to talk about her father.

The children then went on to talk about all the people at school and at home that they could talk to when they were feeling sad or anything else. This list included all the staff at the school, their family, their friends and Ketiwe. The boy who suggested that they could talk to their friends, looked at S while saying it. When they had all said goodbye to Ketiwe, and only S remained, the educational psychologist put Ketiwe's face next to his cheek and she 'kissed' him goodbye. S was told that she wanted to say goodbye to him specially and he replied, 'That's coz she knows how I feel.' He then waved goodbye to her.

This session nearly had me in tears, the teacher actually cried. S had not spoken to anyone (including his father or other family members) since his mother passed away. It really made me so proud to be involved with something so powerful!

I passionately believe that when the Dolls are used by committed adults and embedded in an anti-discriminatory and culturally appropriate curriculum, they can and do change children's perceptions, attitudes and behaviour. But believing in their power is not enough. A body of convincing evidence from recent research projects validates what was previously speculation. It is with great pleasure that I describe them in chapter 7.

There are many examples in this book that will encourage children, even at the foundation stage, to become critical thinkers, explorers and agents of change. It is important that they should because as Epstein (1993) argues:

'[It] is essential to view every school as a site of struggle, where the negotiations taking place can either strengthen or weaken possibilities for developing education for equality.'

The Quality Curriculum Authority (QCA) and legislation including the *Race Relations Amendment Act (2000), the Disability Discrimination Act (2005) and the Children Acts (1989 and 2004)* require that educators focus on promoting equality and develop strategies to close the gap between those children who are achieving and those who are not. Unfortunately, not all have the confidence, skills and knowledge they need to put these obligations into practice. Freire (1994:9) wrote: 'One of the tasks of the progressive educator ... is to unveil opportunities for hope, no matter what the obstacles might be.'

Resistance to addressing discriminatory issues is a hard nut to crack. As Christian Schiller reminds us: 'Acts of Parliament change names and they change procedures but they do not change people ... It is only people who create or allow change.'

Terminology

I use the term educator to refer to all adults, whatever their qualifications, who work with and encourage children to enjoy finding out about the world and its people. Included are childminders, playgroup workers, nursery nurses, teachers, learning support staff, lecturers and residential care workers.

I use the term Black to refer to people of African, Caribbean or Asian origin who experience racism and are most immediately perceived as 'Black' by White people and so includes adults and children in mixed parentage families. The term also refers to those who are seen as 'non-white' who may experience prejudice and differential treatment because of their ethnicity, such as people with Arab, Cypriot, or Latin American cultures and backgrounds. This political definition was formulated to unite people of diverse origins and cultures in the fight against racism and at the same time to reflect the reality that a range of ethnic groups are affected even though they are not equally targeted. Some may not see themselves as allies in a struggle against racism and may even be members of the British National Party. The first letters of the terms Black and White are written in capitals to draw attention to the fact that they are being used as political terms. Although not everyone will agree with the way I have defined and explained the terms I've used, I hope I have not caused offence.

The following poem was written by a pupil from King Edward School Birmingham. The sentiments expressed will probably strike a chord with many readers:

Fair Dinkum!
Dear White Fella
coupla tings you should know
When I born, I black
When I grow up, I black
When I go in the sun, I black
When I cold, I black
When I scared, I black
When I sick, I black
And when I die
I still black.
You White Fella
When you born, you pink
When you grow up, you white
When you go in the sun, you red
When you cold, you blue
When you scared, you yellow
When you sick, you green
And when you die, you grey.
And you have the cheek
to call me coloured!

(anon)

1

Equality is at the heart of quality education

Settings and schools that implement anti-discriminatory education are at the same time providing high quality education. The two are inter-linked: you can't have one without the other. Moreover, embedding equality principles is fast becoming obligatory and no longer a question of individual choice. It is heartening to see that the Department for Children, Schools and Families (DCSF) and the Qualifications and Curriculum Authority (QCA) through their statutory and non-statutory policies, guidelines and schemes of work are prioritising inclusion and equality for the foundation stage and at key stages 1 and 2.

Some examples:
The revised National Curriculum (2000) urges educators to meet the needs of every child: so that each has the opportunity to blossom:

> When planning, teachers should set high expectations and provide opportunities for all pupils to achieve, including boys and girls, pupils with special educational needs, pupils with disabilities, pupils from all social and cultural backgrounds, pupils of different ethnic groups including travellers, refugees and asylum seekers, and those from diverse linguistic backgrounds. Teachers need to be aware that pupils bring to school different experiences, interests and strengths which will influence the way in which they learn.

The KEEP (Key Elements of Effective Practice) principles are designed to guide reflective practice. They link directly with inclusive anti-discriminatory education because through initial and ongoing training and development educators are encouraged to develop, demonstrate and continually improve their:

■ relationships with both children and adults

■ understanding of the individual and diverse ways that children develop and learn

■ knowledge and understanding to actively support and extend children's learning in and across all areas and aspects of learning

■ ability to meet all children's needs, learning styles and interests

■ work with parents and the wider community

■ work with other professionals within and beyond the setting

Some of the principles identified in the QCA's Curriculum Guidance for the Foundation Stage (2000) and considered necessary to achieve high quality care and education, are basic anti-discriminatory principles:

■ no child should be excluded or disadvantaged because of his or her 'race', culture or religion, home language, family background, special educational needs, disability, gender or ability

■ educators need to ensure that all children feel included, secure, and valued. They must build positive relationships with parents in order to work effectively with them and their children

■ children, parents and educators must work together in an atmosphere of mutual respect.

SEAL (Social and Emotional Aspects of Learning) underpins PSHCE Personal, Social, Health and Citizenship Education and includes similar activities to those suggested to encourage reflection and critical thinking on page 70.

The QCA/DfES schemes of work for Citizenship at key stages 1 and 2 also mirror the inclusive anti-discriminatory approach to education. Educators are required to encourage children to develop the knowledge, skills and understanding they need to challenge racism and positively value people who are different from themselves. They are advised to use materials that reflect social and cultural diversity and to provide positive images of 'race', gender and disability.

The UN Convention on the Rights of the Child (1989) has been ratified by Britain. The principles embodied in it also mirror those that underpin an anti-discriminatory approach. The preamble to this powerful document states that:

> ... children should be brought up in the spirit of the ideas proclaimed in the charter of the United Nations, and in particular in the spirit of peace, dignity, tolerance, freedom, equality and solidarity.

There are 54 Articles of rights. Most relevant here is Article 29 which states that the education of the child shall be directed to:

- giving the pupil the possibility to develop in his or her own way and according to his or her ability

- teaching a respect for human rights and freedoms and the principles of the UN

- developing respect for the pupil's cultural identity, language and values and for cultures different from his or her own

- preparing the pupil for a responsible life as an adult in a free society in a spirit of understanding, peace, tolerance, equality of the sexes and friendship among all peoples

- teaching the pupil respect for the natural environment.

Britain has also ratified the *UN Convention on the Rights of People with Disabilities* (2006). Article 24, 2b requires states to ensure that disabled children 'can access an inclusive, quality, primary and secondary education on an equal basis with others in the communities in which they live.'

Implementing anti-discriminatory education is a professional requirement because unfair treatment based on prejudice harms children's development and limits their potential. It includes identifying and breaking down barriers to participation, belonging and achievement. When implemented, the delivery of improved outcomes for all children and the closing of the achievement gap between those who are disadvantaged and others, have a greater chance of success. Educators encourage children to be curious and motivated to learn about the world around them. Do they not also have a responsibility to help them unlearn any prejudices, stereotypical thinking, misconceptions and discriminatory behaviour they may have absorbed?

The Report of the Stephen Lawrence Inquiry (Macpherson, 1999) drew attention to the fact that from an early age children start noticing and learning about the differences and the similarities between people. But this is not all they do. They gradually learn about and develop positive – and negative – attitudes towards people who are different from and similar to themselves by observing the actions, reactions, body language and words of adults and children in the world around them. This process is reinforced by the images they see in books, on packaging and on television. As children are active participants in this learning process the extent to which they absorb these messages will depend on factors like their ethnicity, personality, social class, the attitudes and behaviour they witness in their homes and in the settings or schools they attend. Iram Siraj-Blatchford and Priscilla Clarke (2000:5) point out that the children's perceptions of themselves also play a part:

> ... every girl or disabled child does not perceive themselves in the same way. In fact, children from structurally disadvantaged groups often hold contradictory positions, which is why we might find in our classrooms Black and other ethnic minority children who are very confident and academically successful in spite of the structural, cultural and interpersonal racism in society. Similarly, we will find working class boys who do not conform to a stereotype and are caring and unaggressive and African Caribbean boys who are capable and well-behaved.

Educators can contribute to breaking the cycle by which White children learn to be racists and Black children suffer: a cycle that has tragic consequences as illustrated by the killing of Stephen Lawrence.

Does multicultural education provide the key?
Multicultural education dates back to the 1970s. It was based on the theory that if White children were given opportunities to learn about others cultures, they would become less racially prejudiced and if Black children were able to see their culture reflected in their settings and schools, their self-esteem and sense of belonging would rise leading to greater academic success. This approach has had a huge impact on practice. Today Christian festivals are not the only ones celebrated, school dinners include dishes from various cultures while in role-play areas children 'cook and eat' foods with unfamiliar utensils that are normal for others. In the dressing up area children can now wear clothes like those their parents wear while others have the opportunity

4

to wear unfamiliar clothes like *salwar kamize* and *salwar kurta, saris* and Chinese traditional dress. In settings and schools across the country educators can draw on a range of educational resources and books that reflect many cultures in a variety of languages. Celebrating festivals and learning about cultures which are different from their own can be fun, can extend children's general knowledge and vocabulary and can offer parents an opportunity to participate and make a valuable contribution. All these innovations are to be welcomed. However, although the conviction that multicultural education by itself can raise Black children's chances of academic success or can change White children's attitudes is definitely a step in the right direction, I believe it does not go far enough:

- multicultural education fails to acknowledge the impact of racism and the deeply rooted hierarchy of cultures that exists in Britain. White middle class cultures tend to be highly regarded while Black cultures, White and Black working class cultures tend to be less valued

- It is also questionable whether simply learning about cultures and appreciating cultural differences: the way other people do things and the way 'they' celebrate 'their' festivals, actually impinge on negative attitudes that children might already hold towards adults and children from these cultures.

It may in fact embarrass rather than raise the self-esteem and achievement of children from the particular culture being spotlighted as this example from Burgess-Macey and Crichlow (1996) illustrates:

> A teacher had planned that the children would make and eat samosas. When a White child refused to take part in the activity because this was 'paki' food the teacher did not know how to respond and simply reprimanded the child, 'Don't be rude'. The child then departed for another activity leaving the teacher feeling uncomfortable and Asian children in the group feeling upset, quite possibly wishing that the activity had been to make sandwiches.

- Giving children snapshot impressions of various cultures runs the risk of encouraging crude stereotypes such as that all Chinese people run restaurants, eat with chopsticks and work hard. Apart from misinforming everyone, descriptions like this could anger, hurt and bewilder children from the culture being represented

- The final and most crucial argument is that although it is vital that educators encourage respect for, reflect and promote cultural diversity, these are insufficient on their own.

To be effective, multicultural education has to be embedded in an anti-discriminatory framework so that children can be helped to develop positive attitudes and unlearn any negative ones they have absorbed. In settings and schools in which structures and policies, every day practices and attitudes are designed to promote equality and belonging, children feel at home, are curious about and interested in people similar to and different from themselves and have a positive attitude to learning.

Using Persona Dolls can help educators move from multicultural practice with its focus on resources, diversity, celebrating festivals and displays to anti-discriminatory practice which involves thinking about and ensuring that all instances of stereotypical thinking, prejudice, discrimination and inequality are challenged. The following principles underpin anti-discriminatory education ie high quality education and mirrors what many educators are doing in settings and schools across the country:

- thinking critically and being continually aware of how personal values, assumptions, beliefs and attitudes impinge on good quality practice

- ensuring that all families and children know they are welcome and valued in a setting or school.

Token practices will not convince anyone as this quote from Newstead (2006:48) illustrates:

> ....we can put up as many 'welcome' posters as we have wall space in our settings, but if we are thinking, feeling and doing things that make other people feel uncomfortable about who they are, then all the blue-tack simply goes to waste.

- providing non-stereotypical resources that reflect children from a wide range of ethnic and cultural groups ensures that all parents and their children see their way of life acknowledged and valued: a positive experience for everyone

- continually monitoring and evaluating resources to ensure that no racist, sexist, class, ableist and homophobic messages are being conveyed

- closely observing children and getting to know them as individuals with their own needs, personalities and aspirations

- it also provides opportunities to hear and see instances of prejudice and discrimination that might otherwise pass unnoticed and un-acknowledged

- intervening at appropriate times and in ways that sensitively support and build children's confidence, trust and self-esteem deepens and consolidates their learning and helps them develop new skills and knowledge

- being proactive and challenging stereotypes, assumptions and pre-judices when and wherever they appear.

We all have them in our heads but we need to be aware of them and see them for what they are. Making assumptions about people and stereotyping them are two sides of the same coin. When we see and judge others through prejudiced eyes, our preconceived opinions tend to get in the way and we relate not to the actual person in front of us but to an image in our heads

- expecting children to achieve according to their ability includes being aware that assessments can be based on impressions and assumptions.

Hill and Cole (2001:105) describe the child who pleases:

> The 'nice' child is one who appears to be middle class, or who appears to be able and willing to cease exhibiting working-class, or Islamic or Rasta characteristics, and to adopt those of the white or assimilated middle class. In other words, the 'nice child' is usually one who also meets stereotypes of gender, ethnicity and sexuality.

- treating some children differently to ensure they are treated equally. Fairness does not mean giving everyone equal treatment all the time. Sometimes it involves giving some children special attention, such as those with sensory or physical impairments to ensure that they feel included and can contribute to the group

■ questioning everything – what is being done, why it's being done, what should be retained and what changed.

Many educators, policy makers and researchers explore equality and social justice implications through questioning how some ways of thinking and acting appear normal, appropriate and right while others seem abnormal, inappropriate and wrong. For instance, what is considered 'normal' and what is not, what knowledge is silenced and whose knowledge is privileged, who benefits and how they benefit. Questions like these have motivated educators to rethink and deepen their understandings of equality and to develop and change practice.

■ ensuring that the range of activities provided are appropriate to the age, interests and abilities of the children and that they reinforce and deepen their general knowledge, encourage sustained thinking and foster communication

■ promoting equality of opportunity and a positive attitude to diversity, whether or not there is a diverse population locally, or whether the setting and school caters for a particular religious community.

The Education Regulations for Independent Schools requires that faith schools and settings must consider how to encourage children to respect their own and other cultures in a way that promotes understanding and harmony. It includes being sensitive and tuned in to the feelings of every child and especially to those who are at risk of being bullied and excluded. Responding to all manifestations of unfairness, prejudice and discrimination is essential.

■ listening to children and giving them lots of opportunities to express their thoughts and feelings, ask questions and empathise with others

■ ensuring that they all feel comfortable and that their contributions are acknowledged and valued: that the voices of the more articulate and self-assured don't drown the less assertive children in the group or those not fluent in the dominant language

■ ensuring that the languages of all the children are respected and acknowledged and that their ability to use more than one language is praised. Monolingual children benefit from seeing languages other than English being valued in this way

■ communicating with children learning English as an additional language (EAL) includes learning to read and respond to their body language and to their gestures as well as to their spoken language

■ introducing and developing themes in a variety of ways such as through discussion, art and craft activities, music, stories, books and displays.

Using drama and role-play to highlight fair and unfair situations, similarities and differences and giving children opportunities to express their feelings in a safe setting. Finding out what it feels like to be in someone else's shoes encourages empathy and can stimulate lively discussion.

■ giving opportunities to children to play in a safe and stimulating environment with caring adults. This is essential for all children but even more important for those whose development is delayed.

They need time, encouragement and opportunities to explore experiment and join in activities. A well-planned accessible curriculum enriches the quality of their learning, boosts self-confidence and enables them to experience success whether they are high flyers or find learning difficult. The layout of the room should enable everyone to participate in the day-to-day activities

■ being helped to make the most of their abilities can boost all children's self-awareness, self-esteem and a sense of their own identity and encourage them to explore, express and communicate their needs, feelings and opinions. It is vital that educators and parents work closely together

■ drawing on parents' expertise can help educators gain an understanding of each child's personality, likes and dislikes, abilities and disabilities.

In his article, 'Raise your game', Professor Tony Bertram (2007:10) agrees:

High-quality settings are stimulating, safe and secure and encourage children to explore and construct meaning in an atmosphere that is supportive and challenging. ... Research suggests that the key variable in improving quality and raising outcomes for children is the competent, reflective, well-qualified practitioner who interacts with carer or parent and encourages and supports parents in their aspirations and achievement strategies.

■ maximising the inclusion and involvement of parents by consulting with, listening to and learning from them.

Taking care not to stereotype and devalue their skills, experience and knowledge especially as many are juggling with constant demands on their time and the pressures of everyday life while performing a number of, often conflicting, roles. Some parents may disagree with the anti-discriminatory approach of the setting or school which can be challenging for everyone involved. Derman-Sparks *et al* (1989) reminds us that:

> ... our society gives people permission to use racism, sexism or ablism as outlets for frustration, anger, greed and fear. These facts do not make the bias OK but they help us to look at the whole person and not just at the biased behaviour... Engage the parents in exploring their fears about what may happen to their child as a consequence of anti-bias education and in exploring your ideas about the benefits. Remember that this is a dialogue, not a monologue; make sure that parents have ample opportunity to express their views and that you are open to learning from their views as well as hoping they will learn from yours.

■ using Persona Dolls to help children at the foundation stage and at key stages 1 and 2 acquire the knowledge, understanding and skills they need to counter unfair opinions, attitudes and behaviour. However, to achieve this, they have to unlearn any discriminatory messages they may have absorbed: subtle as well as obvious messages suggesting that White customs, traditions and way of life are the 'right ones' and that it is 'better' to be male than female.

Case Study

The following effective equalities practice was planned and developed by Marisa Barnett in Islington. The impetus for the work developed because two Black girls of African-Caribbean heritage, and two White British girls aged between 3 and 4 years old were excluding L, a child of African-Caribbean and White British mixed parentage. Hurtful comments to her included:

'We don't like you, you're not like us, go away', 'You don't look like us, are you brown or what?' 'Your mum isn't the same colour as you', and 'You haven't got a mum, that's your pretend mum'.

Focused observations showed that L always played alone or with the boys.

It was decided that the most effective way to encourage the children to discuss issues such as discrimination and being excluded was to work with Persona Dolls, as a whole-team strategy. INSET on using the Dolls was run with all the staff.

The Doll, Pia, was introduced to the children who quickly empathised with her, were very interested in the stories told about her, became more confident to give their opinions and come up with ideas and solutions to any problems she 'told' them about. The story Marisa created focused on Pia feeling unhappy and excluded and included negative comments about skin colour. The children responded by naming the emotions Pia was likely to be feeling and L's comments in particular showed that she seemed to identify with Pia and the circumstances of the story.

In the subsequent group discussion the children suggested things that Pia could do about her situation. Ideas from the children were recorded: they included, 'she could tell her mum', 'the children could all play dressing up together' and 'they could sit next to each other at lunch time'.

They drew pictures in which the children, including L, became very involved and worked together. That day at lunchtime, one of the girls chose L to sit next to her.

For a further six weeks follow-up sessions were carried out with the same group of children and a range of strategies were developed to complement the Persona Doll stories. The book, *Through My Window* (1986) became the starting point for discussions on the different make-up of families. Marisa made a family book with photos of the children and their parents and initiated discussions about different family groupings and what colour children were likely to be if their parents were a different colour from each other. Children discussed the different shades of their skin and discovered that there were many shades of brown! They then did some paint mixing to test their theories and answer questions such as 'are people grey?'

Marisa spoke regularly with the parents involved and all were fully supportive of the team's strategies. Interestingly, a mum of one of the African Caribbean girls highlighted her daughter's lack of experience of mixed parentage children which further demonstrated to the staff the importance of exploring issues of equality and diversity with young children.

Celebrating cultural and religious festivals

Learning about a range of festivals is one way to help children move away from ethnocentrism to an awareness of other people's lifestyles. When festivals are presented in an antiracist framework, children's misinformation, stereotypes and prejudices are likely to be expressed and their critical thinking encouraged. Children can see that people celebrate different festivals that honour events and beliefs unique to their ethnic group, that similar themes that run through many festivals, such as renewal, light and darkness, liberation and harvest. Festivals can relate events in the past to present day activities. For instance as part of their celebration of Shavuot when it is believed that God gave the Torah to the Jewish people, children at a reform synagogue nursery in North London made up their own ten commandments for their nursery.

At staff meetings everyone needs to think about why their setting or school is celebrating particular festivals and not others, and how they celebrate them. Parents and others in the community need to be consulted – as well as books, cultural centres and libraries – to ensure that the celebration of the festivals offers children accurate information and does not perpetuate stereotypes. To reflect children's home practices appropriately, educators need to know which festivals their families celebrate, how they celebrate them and whether they would like them to be celebrated in the setting or school, and in what way. Some parents may feel that children should celebrate within their own community and not outside it. By incorporating parents' wishes, the festival activities will support what children learn at home. Discussions can reveal the differences and similarities in the way families who share a religion practice it, and highlight the fact that some families do not practice any religion.

Using the Dolls to describe the different ways in which festivals are celebrated can encourage children to share how they celebrate in their own homes and to realise that theirs isn't the right or only way. For example, a story could be told about how a Hindu Doll's family celebrates Diwali, whether or not there are Hindu children in the group, and the same Doll could tell a story about her friend whose family is also Hindu but who doesn't celebrate Diwali.

On the questionnaire in chapter 8, one teacher recounted a discussion that took place in a school in Blackburn where all the children were from Muslim families:

> When I introduced our Doll to the children in Year 2 and described his typical day, I mentioned that he had his tea at six o'clock. The children wondered why he was not at the Mosque at that time. We then had a discussion revolving around the fact that not everyone goes to Mosque, and talked about other forms and places of worship.

During her interview a teacher in a children's centre also with mainly Muslim children explained how they involve parents:

> This year our focus in the Centre has been on parental involvement and we have made a big thing of celebrating festivals and inviting parents. They've always come in for Eid and Christmas, but this year we've had them in for Diwali and Chinese New Year as well. As part of each festival I told a Persona Doll story using an appropriate Doll and involving some of our other Dolls. For example, when I told the story about Chinese New Year woven around Mei Ling, three of the Dolls were part of the audience: Polly around whom I had told a story at Christmas, Chandeep around whom I had told a story at Diwali and Shabaz around whom I had told a story at Eid. Parents could see the similarities as well as the differences and it went really well. The children knew the Dolls so they could join in and say what happened and I think the parents really enjoyed it. One parent wrote in the front of the child's record of achievement that it was really wonderful the way we were using the Dolls to introduce different cultures. I don't really think that parents look all that much at the display in the hall, but we do talk about the use of the Dolls in the newsletter.

The stories the Dolls tell can help to broaden children's general knowledge and correct misconceptions they may have about other people's festivals. They can encourage older children to consider the commercialisation of festivals and to focus instead on the giving, caring, moral, sharing aspects. A Black Persona Doll could be used to tell the children how her/his family celebrates *Kwanza*: a Swahili word meaning 'first fruits of the harvest'. Kwanza celebrates Black people's African heritage and the principles of unity, community and family that helped their ancestors endure slavery and oppression.

In many settings and schools Mother's Day and Father's Day cards and sometimes gifts are made with the children. When deciding whether or not to celebrate these events educators need to think about single-parent families, those where there are two mothers or two fathers and about looked after children.

Dau (1996:128) reminds us that some children have little to celebrate:

> The children in our early childhood services who come from homes where there is love and gentleness may be willing and enthusiastic to make cards for Father's Day or Mother's Day. If a child comes from a home where there is warfare and violence, how does this child feel when asked to celebrate either of these days? Children need choice about what they celebrate.

Nelson Mandela, Founder and Chairperson of the Nelson Mandela Children Fund, believes that: 'If enough people are touched and imbued with a spirit of caring – we could change the whole landscape of how children are treated.'

2

Dolls with a difference make a difference

Children make judgements about people they perceive as being the same or different from themselves and about the groups they do belong to and about those they don't. In the process they develop a sense of their own identity. These judgements and perceptions are likely to be influenced by prevailing attitudes expressed, by adults, other children, books, television and computer games. They learn that some differences are valued and some are not and that it is OK to treat certain groups of people unequally. They may retain this misinformation for the rest of their lives unless active steps are taken to counter it. Educators and Persona Dolls are powerful so they are in a strong position to challenge these attitudes and equip children to stand up for themselves and others.

Even children whose own lives are happy and secure are likely to know about injustice and unfairness in the world around them from television, from discussions in school and at home. For others, life may consist of harsh realities and complex relationships. Prejudice and racism cause them to feel unsafe and afraid. They may need support to reinforce a strong group and personal identity and prevent them from internalising the negative messages they receive from the world around them. The Dolls and their stories can provide this support and reassurance. During an Ofsted visit to a school in Leicester the inspectors asked to see a Persona Doll session as they had read so much about the strategy. The foundation stage teacher presented a scenario based on a racist incident – the children were completely engaged and the lesson was rated excellent.

The Persona Doll approach offers an effective, stimulating, non-threatening and enjoyable way to combat discrimination, foster emotional literacy, raise equality issues and empower children. By encouraging them to empathise with the Dolls, to 'walk in each other's shoes' and by creating a supportive and co-operative learning environment children are reminded that there are rules about treating each other fairly and with respect. Hopefully, as a result they will transfer this learning to interactions outside the setting and school.

The Dolls were first used in the United States by Kay Taus. At that time, the 1950s, very few resources represented the ethnic composition of the children in her nursery school. Kay and her colleague Ruth moaned and groaned about this unfair and unacceptable situation and one day they took action. They created dolls out of card and to encourage the children to identify and bond with them, they matched their skin colours and physical features as accurately as they could with those of the dolls. Personas were developed for each one and stories based on children's experiences, woven around the dolls – and Persona Dolls were born. According to Taus (1987):

> Persona Dolls are different because they have individual identities just like children in the classroom do. They have a family, they live in a certain town, in a particular house or apartment building, they have certain friends, and these things don't change.

The aim is to help children appreciate the hurt that unfair prejudiced attitudes and discriminatory behaviour cause and, crucially, to develop the skills they need to be able to stand up for themselves and others when faced with unfairness and prejudice.

Educators use the Dolls and their stories to promote PSHCE and extend children's intellectual horizons. The stories enable them to develop children's general knowledge, encourage them to share their cultural traditions and learn about those of their friends, to recognise and challenge stereotypes and enjoy the experience of being part of a creative and stimulating group activity.

Many settings and schools have a range of Dolls to reflect all the children as well as representing groups that are not present. A setting or school may have a Sikh Doll but no Sikh children. The children will thus encounter a wide range of equally valued and respected lifestyles, cultures, languages and abilities.

Encouraging children to respect and value differences and to take a stand against unfairness and injustice is likely to be more effective if educators have some idea of what children have experienced, what they think and what they know about social inequalities. Discussions, debates, project work and Persona Doll storytelling sessions help to provide this information. Care is taken not to reinforce stereotypes when selecting Dolls, developing their personas or creating their stories.

Building personas

Persona Dolls are not ordinary Dolls on which children impose their own imaginations; nor are they puppets. Educators give them their own individual personas and in the process change them from being inanimate objects into 'people' with individual personalities, family, cultural and class backgrounds, names, gender and ages. Most children quickly bond, identify and empathise with the Dolls, sharing their happiness and their sadness. This is what two educators said about Persona Dolls when being interviewed for the evaluation project described in chapter 8:

> The thing about the Dolls is that we create a sort of aura about them. The children then learn to respect them and to realise that they are not like the other dolls that they might throw around.

> I remember once I just had two children with me and the Doll. We were playing outside though it was quite a cold day. One of the children went inside, found a cardigan, came back and put it on the Doll: clearly demonstrating her empathy and concern.

To ensure that the personas they create are detailed and authentic, educators include important facts like where the Dolls live and sleep, the language(s) they speak, their likes and dislikes; the things they are good at and the ones they find difficult, the things that make them happy and those that upset, frighten and worry them, the length of time

17

the family has been in this county, if relevant, and its refugee or Gypsy/ Traveller experiences. When developing personas especially for Dolls from cultures with which educators are unfamiliar, they make sure that they give them appropriate names and pronounce them correctly.

As part of the research described in chapter 7 educators created a Gypsy/ Traveller persona for their Doll because quite a few fairs pass through the county and they thought the children were likely to see Gypsy/ Travellers or hear comments about them. To ensure that the persona was realistic, they first consulted a range of books and then visited Appleby Fair. The photographs, artefacts and the conversations they had had with Gypsy/Travellers were shared with the children through the Doll. The children were fascinated by the fairground roundabout and how it fitted onto the lorry belonging to the Doll's dad. Talking about the Romany language prompted a little boy to compare it with his grandparents' Greek language. They discussed the Doll's trailer and how he lives in different places. A child commented that his own house was glued down onto the ground. The children shared information about their favourite foods and the food you can get at fairs.

One of the educators noted the children's strong emotional engage-ment and how they were able to talk about, share and describe their feelings, especially when the Doll told the children about being bullied. The bullies said he didn't have a proper home, that he was dirty and they pushed him and he pushed them back. To reassure the Doll, one of the children said that he was not to feel sad because 'he had to do it'. The children talked about their home life and were helped to appreciate that families are in some ways different from and in other ways, the same.

Once children and students on teacher training and childcare courses have been introduced to lots of Dolls and heard their stories, they can help to create the persona for a Doll they have not met before:

> The Doll is placed where everyone can see it. The younger children could do this as a brainstorming exercise, answering and discussing appropriate questions. Older ones could work in small groups with somebody in each group writing down their responses.
>
> Some trigger questions:

How old is the Doll?

Is it a boy or a girl?

What is the Doll's name?

What language(s) does the Doll 'speak'?

What makes the Doll happy, sad, cross?

Is the Doll scared of anything?

Where does the Doll live? eg in a flat, house, trailer, temporary accommodation?

Who does the Doll live with?

What jobs do the Doll's parent(s) have? Or is one or both unemployed?

Does the Doll sleep in its own room or does it share a room?

At school what subjects is the Doll good at and which ones, if any, does it find difficult?

At home what does the Doll like doing?

Are there things that it can't do – it's not old enough or because it has a disability?

Are there days of special significance in the Doll's life? How are they spent?

Has anything happened in the Doll's life or about to happen we should know about?

During the feedback somebody from each group presents their Doll to the rest of the class and is questioned by them.

A lecturer explains how and why she encourages students to develop personas and stories:

> I get my students to research various cultures and religions and to then choose a Doll, create a persona for her/him and to think about a potential problem that could arise for the Doll. They then develop a story around this that would engage children in a positive way. This activity develops student's understanding of the need to always address issues of unfairness.

The hotseating technique could be used to explore and create a persona with older children and students who are familiar with the approach.

> The educator sits in a chair with the Doll on his/her lap. The children's and the student's task is to find out as much as they can about the Doll by asking relevant questions. But before replying, the educator needs to continuously 'consult' the Doll to get the information about itself that the children and students are asking about. It is important to remember that as Persona Dolls are not puppets – the educator uses her/his normal speaking voice.

Not everyone feels confident to use the Dolls. This is clear from comments made by some of the educators interviewed for the evaluation project described in chapter 8. The head teacher of a children's centre admitted that:

> You do feel a bit of a fool talking to a Doll sitting on your lap. Certainly some of the younger members of staff find it hard. There is that initial period of just tuning into the Dolls, why you are using them and how you are using them, being comfortable with them. I think people sometimes just think 'oh if we're using Persona Dolls, we're dealing with issues and I'm not comfortable. I don't know what to say.' It's just a question of starting off with the Dolls coming to visit and talking about their lives and gaining confidence to use them to explore issues.

A nursery teacher suggests that:

> You have to be a bit of an actress – it's all about the delivery because if you don't deliver it right, the children won't believe it.

Two managers felt it wasn't right to expect people lacking confidence to use the Dolls. One stated:

> Adults have to believe that the Dolls are special people – it's not easy for everyone to do. ... I would not ask my staff to do it if they weren't confident. It would ruin it, ruin the magic.

And the other agreed:

> We try to keep it that only people who feel confident and comfortable use the Dolls. I will take the lead and model their use when needed.

When being interviewed as part of this project, two of the educators drew attention to the fact that personas need to be written down and that the Dolls must be properly stored:

> The most important thing is to record the personas, keep them with the Doll they refer to and then add subsequent stories and the children's responses. It's finding the time to do this that's hard. I'm lucky, my learning support assistant often types them up for me. The children always remember all the details so you have to get the story straight. I told a story in which the Doll had six brothers and the children remembered all their names!

> In the Persona Doll cupboard there is a space for each Doll and her/his journal. Recently the senior teacher has added sheets of possible scenarios

which link to the SEAL curriculum areas. This means that the Dolls are easily accessible and there is a bank of ideas for staff to use.

Storytelling sessions

Persona Dolls and their stories can boost children's confidence, self-esteem, identity formation and motivation to learn. During the interactive, informal problem-solving sessions, educators have high expectations of each and every child and support is offered to those experiencing physical or verbal abuse from other children or adults.

The sessions encourage children to feel good about their own cultural and family backgrounds while at the same time respecting, valuing and learning about the cultural and family backgrounds of the rest of the group. Talking about these similarities and differences can help them understand that being different is not something to tease or harass each other about.

The children's active engagement, their bonding and concern for the Doll and the adult's supportive facilitation ensure in the words of Wood and Atfield (1996) that the sessions are hands-on and brain-on. They become decision makers and problem-solvers, a role that helps boost reasoning, reflection, self-esteem and confidence. The empathy that is built-up between them and the Dolls can help them appreciate the hurt that prejudiced attitudes and discriminatory behaviour inflicts. It makes the stories more real if the Dolls do not always behave like angels.

Many of the stories raise issues of justice, equality, discrimination and struggle and deepen children's understanding of fairness and unfairness. Through their identification with the Dolls children are helped to see the injustice of the situations the stories describe and are motivated to think of solutions to the problems the Dolls tell them about.

Educators speak for the Doll and in their role as facilitator guide the session by asking scaffolding questions to capture the children's interest and, crucially, to make connections between what is known and unknown. They encourage the children to reflect critically on what they and their peers have said, to use language to structure their thoughts. Accepting and acknowledging that some children's ideas about the right way to act and interact will not match theirs, most educators check that they don't unconsciously respond more positively to the children who are most like them. They are aware that verbal and non-verbal communication is governed by cultural rules. The body language that children from various ethnic and cultural backgrounds learn may be different from their own. For example, many Black children are taught that looking at an older person straight in the eye is disrespectful and impolite whereas many White children are taught to look directly at an adult when they are spoken to: a sign of frankness and honesty.

If they feel safe, secure and comfortable with the educator and their peers, children are more likely to contribute their ideas, feelings and experiences. Given this encouragement, educators may be surprised by what children say: their powers of observation and understanding of the world around them are often under-estimated.

By presenting a range of scenarios and problems for children to assess, explore and solve, the Dolls through the stories they tell, open up a world of possibilities and encourage children to imagine what it might be like to live through situations that they have not personally experienced.

Emotional involvement in the stories is crucial because it helps to capture and deepen children's interest, arouse their curiosity and challenge them intellectually. As different stories gradually connect up in their heads, so their understanding of quite complex social issues develops. Their questions and any topics that have captured their interest can be explored in more detail in other areas of the curriculum.

Ginnis and Ginnis (2006) outline some of the ways in which stories contribute to children's emotional intelligence – a role Persona Doll stories are designed to play. They suggest that stories provide:

- personal awareness: what am I like in comparison to others: they hold up a mirror to oneself

- an understanding of how relationships function – what builds them, what destroys them and how they might be repaired

- models of behaviours, both good and bad, in a whole range of situations as characters react to widely ranging circumstances

- an understanding that all behaviours are choices and all choices have consequences – this is the foundation stone of a personally responsible approach to life

- a view of how communities such as families and friendships operate – the importance of give and take, of social responsibility, of agreed rules and of routines

- insights into major human themes, such as conflict, trust, betrayal, loyalty, justice, greed, honesty, power, love, hate, guilt, happiness and sadness – the list is almost endless

- a catalogue of recognisable and named emotions and feelings

- the beginnings of a wide world-view and an incipient understanding of human nature

Closed questions could lead children who frequently answer incorrectly to see themselves and to be seen by the other children as less competent. It could affect their spontaneity and willingness to express their true feelings and views. On the other hand, skilful open-ended questioning that put children in the role of experts can foster self-esteem, encourage them to consider alternative responses and to think about their own assumptions.

Open-ended questions also develop children's capacity to make up their own minds on issues of fairness. Questions like, 'If you saw what happened to the Doll what would you have done? 'What if' questions can deepen children's involvement and reflection, such as: What if the teacher had seen or heard what happened? What if the Doll had hit back? What if something else had been said or done? Asking questions can expose any misconceptions they may have picked up, or fears and anxieties they are experiencing. Sometimes questions elicit unexpected answers, as happened at this children's centre: a mixed parentage child who was new to the centre was playing in the outdoor area and an Asian boy called her 'Blackie'. The practitioner who heard him dealt with the situation there and then and later used a Persona Doll to talk about name calling and how it makes children feel. This is what happened next:

> I took Joel into the group because the children had met him several times and knew a lot about his life and the happy stories he had told us. They also knew that his mum was White and his dad was Black. I asked the children about Joel to recap their knowledge of him. I then told them that he was very sad today because something had happened at his nursery that he didn't like. The children were keen to know what. I said that he had been

called a nasty name and asked them it that had ever happened to them. The little girl from the playground incident immediately put up her hand. Brilliant, I thought, this is going according to plan! I asked her what she had been called, expecting her response to be 'Blackie'. Instead, it was Muriel!! It made me realise that I need to do more work on name calling and to use appropriate terminology so that children can learn which names are hurtful and nasty and which are acceptable.

Some children need more time to express their thoughts and feelings than others. Their initial silence may not indicate unwillingness to contribute or that they have nothing to contribute. Not talking about something is not the same as not thinking about it and in any case doesn't rule out the possibility of it being expressed at some other time. Children have the right to remain silent and extended silences provide opportunities for them to reflect and extend their thinking. The problem is that silences can cause discomfort and be hard to bear. Silin (2002) appeals to educators to listen carefully to the voices of children and to ensure that in their noisy classrooms silence can emerge. He believes that 'silence opens space for others to announce themselves'. Wise words of great relevance to those facilitating Persona Doll storytelling sessions.

Not all Persona Doll stories are about discrimination and prejudice. Children need to hear stories about happy enjoyable times that the Dolls experience as well as those in which they are physically or emotionally hurt. This is important because children should look forward to the sessions and not approach them with trepidation: what upsetting story are we going to hear today? The Dolls are the children's friends and should not come across as victims. The problem is that many educators anxious to avoid these situations tend to lose sight of anti-discrimination! One solution is to create stories that expand children's understanding and knowledge about cultures different from theirs and to draw parallels.

A few ideas:

- the Doll has had an argument with its parent over what to wear when going to a particular event. It could ask the children if that kind of thing happens to them and what they do about it

- the Doll loves going to mosque, church, synagogue, gurdwara or temple but sometimes gets bored. It could ask the children if this happens to them and what they do if it does

- the Doll doesn't always have to have a problem to solve: the Doll and the children can just have conversations, perhaps about the music they like

- the Doll finds a particular aspect of the curriculum difficult and comes to talk about it

- the Dolls could come and tell the children happy stories that their parents or grandparents have told them about what happened when they were children

- the Doll could tell the children about a memorable event or day

Case Study

The Dolls are used not only to tell stories about things that happen to them but also to trigger a range of learning activities:

Safina, one of the Persona Dolls, was about to turn four. The children were told that she was going to have a birthday party at school just like they have. A range of learning activities was set up, some adult led and others child initiated. A clothes shop was organised in the role-play area. Two of the girls decided to take Safina to the shop and buy her a shalwar and kamize to wear on her birthday. At the shop they measured the clothes on Safina to buy the right size and exchanged money for the purchase. They talked about the colour and whether they wanted plain or patterned before a decision was made.

Many of the children made party hats for themselves, the adults and for all four Persona Dolls. This also involved measurement plus discussions about size, shape, pattern and colour and what material they would use to make the hats out of and how they would fix them together. Schema were also explored as the children enveloped recycled materials in wrapping paper. Invitations and birthday cards were designed by children on the computers and in the mark making areas. Some children were able to copy writing a greeting, others used their own strings of letters to represent meaning.

What should be eaten at a party was decided by the children. They 'wrote' lists of food and recipes. Their favourite food, sandwiches, pizza, biscuits and birthday cakes were then made. This involved use of fine motor skills with a variety of utensils. The children talked about their actions and made predictions about the changes that might occur in the cooking process.

They played party games outside, some with music and instruments and others with the parachute. They had four actual parties so the children could be involved or not but they could still access the areas in that particular room. They lit four candles four times, counting them first, and sang 'Happy Birthday to Safina' four times. The children danced and played various percussion instruments alongside a range of music tapes: African, Asian and nursery songs. All four Dolls were taken into this area and the children danced with them. It was hard work for the dedicated staff but they all agreed that it was a worthwhile experience for the children. They still look at the book that was made of the day and ask when it's going to be the other Persona Dolls' birthdays.

Close observation and listening to children of all ages can reveal discriminatory attitudes and behaviour that might surprise educators. Once heard or witnessed, the incident needs to be dealt with immediately and then woven into a Persona Doll story. When the scenario is based on an actual incident, the situation needs to be changed and the Doll needs to have a different gender or ethnicity from that of the children involved to prevent the victim and the perpetrator being recognised by their peers.

A great advantage of the Persona Doll approach is that no child is targeted and made to feel bad. They are helped to appreciate the hurt experienced by the Doll and given an opportunity to talk about what they would have done if they were there. It helps to focus children's mind and thoughts on the Doll, a 'person' one step removed, so easier to deal with. Because they identify with and care about the Dolls, children may reflect and reassess their attitudes and behaviour.

3

Story time

I t is recognised in the National Curriculum (2000) that children develop their ability to learn how to learn by practising thinking skills. Educators are therefore encouraged to provide opportunities for children to problem solve, make decisions, predict and critically question – which is precisely what Persona Doll storytelling sessions are designed to develop.

The stories in this book are woven around discriminatory incidents because, judging from our experience and that of other researchers (see chapters 7 and 8), most educators use the Dolls to promote PSHCE but do not to actively challenge inequality and exclusion. This should not obscure the fact that with the help of Persona Dolls, excellent work is being done in settings and schools around the country to promote PSHCE.

Exclusion, prejudice and discriminatory behaviour can make settings or schools feel emotionally unsafe. Children are unlikely to feel good about themselves if they are afraid of being bullied, worried about meeting adult expectations or if they have no friends. To enable children to meet the outcomes of the Every Child Matters agenda, Persona Doll story sessions help to boost children's sense of security, confidence, self-esteem and concentration.

The stories that follow are not intended to be recipes but rather to spark ideas and send strong anti-discriminatory messages. Those that deal with experiences that arouse children's empathy and concern are likely to be the ones they remember, as this anecdote illustrates:

An adviser took a Sikh Persona Doll wearing a salwar kurta with her when she visited a playgroup in west London. She told the children a story about how upset the Doll was because the other children kept teasing him: calling him a girl and saying he was wearing his pyjamas. His friend was ill in bed so he had nobody to play with. The children were interested and involved in the story but the adviser only appreciated the depth of their involvement when she visited them again eight months later, without the Doll. She was greeted with questions about him: were the other children still teasing him? Was his friend back at school? They remembered the Doll's name but not the adviser's!

Children need to hear stories about happy experiences as well as sad ones and be encouraged to talk about their positive and negative emotions. Through hearing lots of Persona Doll stories they may decide that it's good to talk about problems, that it often makes things better: they might even come to the conclusion that some problems can't be solved.

When introducing a Doll to children for the first time, educators normally talk about the most crucial bits of its persona at the first meeting. Through subsequent visits and stories the children gradually learn more about the Doll. This process can't of course be replicated in a book, so many of the personas are described here in detail.

The following examples suggest that Persona Doll stories told by respectful, sensitive and empathetic educators give children appropriate information so they can understand what it feels like to be targeted and be empowered to act. Sometimes the Dolls can be unkind to their friends and not know how to make amends.

Meeting Robyn

This is my new friend. Her name is Robyn. It was her birthday last Tuesday: she turned four. She wants me to tell you about her house. It is near Sainsbury's and she wants to know if anyone lives near her.

[The children respond]

There are seven people in her house – her mum, her dad, her Nan, her sister Jane – she's 10 and her other sister Alice is nearly 8. There's also Tim but he's only a baby. After school and in the holidays when their mum and dad are at work then their Nan looks after them. Their mum is a doctor and their dad works in an office in a very tall building. Robyn says she doesn't exactly know what she does there. Robyn says I must tell you that they never ever cook or eat meat – they're vegetarians. They think it's cruel to kill animals for food. She wants to know if any of you are vegetarian. Her favourite foods are cauliflower cheese, baked potatoes, salad and all kinds of fruit. But she doesn't like eggs!! She wonders what foods you like best.

[The children respond]

Most of the time Robyn and her two sisters, Jane and Alice, are good friends but sometimes they argue. Robyn gets cross when they don't do what she wants to do and when her friend Lizzie comes to play, Robyn gets mad with Alice because she always wants to join in their games, which usually ends with Alice crying.

[The children respond]

Robyn likes school and has quite a lot of friends. She says you can usually find them in the role-play area. She's nearly always the mum and her best friend Lizzie is her little girl. Sometimes they play hospitals and Robyn says she always has to be the doctor because she's the only one whose mum is a doctor.

She asked me to tell you that she's very excited because on Saturday the whole family except her Nan and baby Tim are going to Legoland. She wonders if any of you have been there.

[The children respond]

She has to go now so she says goodbye.

Robyn's story

Do you remember when Robyn visited us last week where she said she was going with her family?

[The children respond]

Robyn told me that they had a fantastic time but do you think she's feeling happy today?

[The children respond]

You're right. Would you like to know why she's so unhappy?

[The children respond]

Robyn says there's a girl called Jeanette in her nursery class. Everyone likes her and wants to be friends with her. Yesterday morning before school started, Lizzie, Robyn's friend arrived with her hair cut very very short. Jeanette laughed at her and chanted, 'Look at Lizzie she's a boy, Look at Lizzie she's a boy.' Robyn and lots of the children joined in pointing and chanting. Lizzie just stood there looking miserable. What do you think Robyn did next?

[The children respond]

No, she didn't. She walked away. Why do you think Robyn did that?

[The children respond]

Usually Robyn's starving hungry when she gets back from school. Not yesterday. And when she went to bed she couldn't sleep – she tossed and turned, tossed and turned. Her tummy felt all funny but she wasn't sick.

She wants to know what you think she should do when she sees Lizzie at school tomorrow?

[The children respond]

What should she do if Lizzie's not at school?

[The children respond]

Robyn says you've given her lots of good ideas and she's feeling happier. She says thank you so much.

Persona Dolls and the stories they tell can support children with disabilities or additional needs, especially if they are in a similar situation. It can be comforting for a child to discover that they are not alone. Children with siblings who have disabilities or additional needs can also find the stories helpful, as this educator reports:

> One of the most powerful instances with the Dolls was with Jessica, a little girl whose sister in Year 3 has Down's syndrome. When Jessica joined the school she was fine but when she got to year 2 she had a real wobbly. She was beginning to realise how different her sister really was. I introduced a Persona Doll who had a little brother who was hard of hearing and had lots of problems: it was important that his situation was not identical to Jessica's. Suddenly Jessica talked all about Charlotte and about her difficulties. I think it was really good for her.

When being interviewed for the Evaluation Project described in chapter 8, a learning support assistant told this story:

> There is a school I work with that has two new Polish children and the teacher overheard some of the children saying that they wouldn't play with the one little boy because he couldn't talk properly. She mentioned this to me and I suggested using the Persona Dolls when I came in. So I wrote a six week plan for developing the story and the children really took to the Doll and came up with lots of ideas for including him in their play. But some-

thing interesting and unexpected also happened in the class. There was a little boy with a condition called hyper-mobility. This meant that he moved very quickly and quite clumsily so that he often bumped into children, and tended to squeeze anything that he got hold of: other children, animals etc. He became very interested in the Doll and learned to hold her very gently and stroke her hair: this really helped him with his interactions with the other children.

If children have never been in close contact with adults or children with disabilities, they may be frightened, anxious and upset when a child with a disability comes to the setting or school. Their knowledge, mis-information, prejudices and fears about disabilities are often revealed through the questions they ask. Educators need to provide the space and time to ask them.

An educator in a children's centre realised that the reason why some of the children did not include Catherine, the only child who used a wheelchair, was that they were worried and fearful. She told a story about a Doll called Anna, to help them see that Anna was like them in many ways but that she was also different from them because she used a walking frame. Being able to voice their feelings and ask questions in a safe and supportive environment helped to allay the children's fears and they began to include Catherine in their games.

Children can tease those who they perceive as being different and less capable. This story was told to a reception class where a little boy was finding it hard to be accepted by the other children: although older than them, he found keeping up difficult.

Lilly's story

Somebody you've never met before has come to visit you today. She's got a problem and doesn't know what she should do about it. She hopes you can help her. But before I tell you about what's worrying her, she wants me to tell you something about herself and her family. Her name is Lillian but everybody calls her Lilly. She's almost 7 and her sister, Susan is 9. They live with their mum in a flat above the shops in the High Street. Their dad lives in a house in Poole and Lilly and Susan sometimes stay with him at weekends and during the holidays. Lilly says she loves being with her dad but she's not so keen on Nicola who lives with him. She shouts at Lilly all the time even when she's not doing anything wrong! How do you think that makes Lilly feel?

31

[The children offer some suggestions]

Lilly's favourite time of the day is .....

[Doll whispers in teacher's ear]

Oh! She wants you to guess.

[The children make suggestions]

Well, it's bedtime. Not because she loves sleeping but because she loves listening to the stories her mum or Susan read to her. Lilly says she can read by herself but it takes her a long time to finish a page.

[Doll whispers in teacher's ear]

Lilly wants to know if any of you find reading hard?

[The children respond]

Actually Lilly finds lots of things hard to do like dressing and undressing. She takes a long time eating even her favourite foods: chips, pasta, chicken nuggets and baked potatoes with lots of grated cheese. She takes even longer when she has to eat foods she doesn't like: fish, cabbage and bananas. Sometimes her mum shouts at her and tells her to hurry-up and Susan often teases her and calls her 'slowcoach'.

How do you think that makes Lilly feel?

[The children respond]

Lilly loves watching TV, playing on the computer and going bowling with her mum and Susan but she doesn't like reading to herself or out loud in class, or doing things like jig-saw puzzles: Susan loves completing them. Lilly says she's no good at sports because she can't run very fast but she's a really good singer and is in the school choir.

[Doll whispers in teacher's ear]

Lilly wants to know what you like doing but she said please don't all talk at the same time because she won't be able to hear what you're saying.

[The children respond]

[Doll whispers in teacher's ear]

Lilly wants to know if you want to hear about her problem?

[The children respond]

There's a new boy in her class called Roger. Yesterday, when they were in the playground, he and his friends followed her around calling her 'Dozy Lilly' and 'Silly Lilly' making sure that the teacher on duty couldn't hear them.

[Doll whispers in teacher's ear]

Lilly says she really really hates being teased like that but doesn't know what to do about it. She wants to know if you were her what would you do?

[The children respond]

[Doll whispers in teacher's ear]

Lilly says thank you so much for all the ideas you've given her. She's not quite so worried about going back to school now.

Thanks to trendy frames, the teasing of children who wear glasses appears to have decreased but it does still happen. A teacher told the children in her reception class the following story because a boy who wears glasses and has been bullied at his present school will be joining the group next term.

Meeting Catlyn

I have a new friend for you to meet today. Her name is Catlyn and she's nearly five years old. She won't be coming to our school but she'll often visit us. She told me that she hopes you'll all be her friends. Next week she is going to her new school and she's a bit worried about it. She wants to know how you felt when you first came to this school and you didn't know anyone? What made you feel better?

[The children respond]

You've never met Catlyn before because her family used to live in Ireland. Last month they moved into a house near the bus station. Catlyn wants me to tell you about her family. She lives with her mum, her dad, and her big sister Brenda. Brenda is eight and Catlyn loves it when they play together but when Brenda's friends come to play she never lets Catlyn join in. She wants to know if that happens to you?

[The children respond]

Catlyn's mum and dad are both nurses at the hospital. Catlyn says she's going to be a nurse when she grows up, or maybe a doctor. She says she's quite good at reading but number-work is hard. Her favourite things are playing in the home area, listening to stories and building with the bricks: but some of the boys say girls can't play with bricks. She doesn't think that's fair. She wants to know what you think.

[The children respond]

Catlyn has a wish. She wishes she could dance like her sister Brenda in beautiful clothes and special shoes. They both go to classes to learn Irish dancing but Catlyn says it's really hard to remember the steps. She wants to know if there are things you wish you could do.

[Children respond]

She says I must tell you that something very exciting is going to happen. The whole family are going to Ireland in an aeroplane to stay on Grandma's and Grandpa's farm. Catlyn loves all the animals but she's a bit scared of the cows and horses – they're so big! Grandma is arranging a picnic and all Catlyn's aunts and uncles and cousins will be coming. She says she'll tell you all about it but she has to go now.

Catlyn's story

Do you remember when Catlyn visited us last week? Do you remember where she was going with her mum and dad and her big sister Brenda?

[The children respond]

What very good memories you've all got. Do you remember the special thing that was going to happen when they were at the farm?

[The children respond]

You're right. Catlyn told me that they had a fantastic picnic: delicious food and her Grandma's special biscuits. She says everyone loved being on the farm and she hopes they'll go there again soon.

As you can see, Catlyn doesn't look happy today. Something horrible happened at her school yesterday. Oh! Catlyn says I must first tell you about the good thing that happened.

Catlyn and her mum went to the optician. Do you know what an optician is? The optician tested her eyes and said she needed glasses. There were lots and lots to choose from and Catlyn picked a frame that looked just like her dad's. She told me she wanted to take them home with her but the optician had laughed and said they weren't proper glasses yet because they didn't have any lenses in them. Do you know what lenses are?

[One of the children explains]

Catlyn said that as soon as her glasses were ready, she and her mum went to fetch them. She says that when she put them on she couldn't believe the

34

difference they made. Everything looked so clear and bright. At home her dad, Nan, grand-dad, and her sister, Brenda, all said how lovely she looked in her new glasses. Her mum took a picture of Catlyn and her dad wearing their glasses. Catlyn told me she couldn't wait to show her glasses to her friends at school.

But when she got to school instead of everyone admiring her glasses and telling her how good she looked, they made a circle around her and chanted, 'Four eyes, four eyes, Catlyn's got four eyes.' How do you think Catlyn felt? Has anything like that ever happened to you? How did you feel?

[The children respond]

Catlyn says things got even worse. Her friends said her glasses weren't cool, that she looked silly in them and they didn't want to play with her. So she just stood by herself. She felt too miserable, upset and disappointed to play. She felt like crying but she was worried they'd call her a cry baby, so she didn't. Her tummy felt all funny. She wonders if you've ever felt like that.

[The children respond]

She wants to know if you can help her. She's really worried about tomorrow. What if the same thing happens? What if they call her names and don't want to play with her? What do you think she should do?

[The children respond]

Catlyn says you've given her lots of good ideas and she's feeling happier. She says thank you so much. When she comes next time would you like her to tell you what happened?

[The children respond]

Educating children with disabilities or additional educational needs alongside their peers in mainstream schools is now recognised as a human right and an equal opportunities issue. When they are educated together in mainstream schools, both abled and disabled children have opportunities to adapt and accommodate each other's needs and to learn new skills. A teacher reported that there is a child with quite severe autism in their nursery school who needs extra help. When she spoke to the mothers of two of the children who are really really good with him, it turned out that they both have uncles with special educational needs. But some of the children complained: 'Why does H get away with it'? 'Why is he allowed to do that and I'm not?' It's quite difficult because autism is a very hard concept for children to grasp: there is nothing there for them to see. The teacher decided it was time for a Persona Doll story. Instead of weaving it around a Doll as she normally did, she decided to tell a story about an autistic friend of one of their Dolls because she felt that a Doll with autism would probably be unable to 'talk' to the children! The story was about the fact that the Doll's friend needed special help because he couldn't understand some things and the children immediately said, 'Oh like H' and they talked about the things they did to help him.

Telling a story about a Persona Doll who uses a wheelchair had an unexpected consequence for one little girl in this Children's Centre:

> The Centre has a range of Dolls that the children know and love. Haroon is one of them. The children had been told that he is 4 years old and lives with his Dad in a bungalow with a big garden but no steps. There is something wrong with his legs so he can't walk or run or hop or climb. Instead he uses a wheelchair. He uses his hands and arms to make it move from room to room and to whizz around in the garden. He can make his wheelchair go so fast that when his friends run races with him, he often wins. He's really good at throwing a football and can get it into a basketball net. He sleeps on a mattress on the floor and with his strong arms he can get in and out of bed.

> When Haroon visited the children after a break of two months, they remembered most of the things they had been told about him, were interested in the story he had come to tell and were engaged during the subsequent discussion. One of the children in the group, Imaan, has left-sided cerebral palsy mainly affecting her left leg. She wears a splint and operates extremely well around the centre, walking, running, climbing. She only needs a pushchair to get from home to school and back again. One day her mum came to fetch her after lunch to take her to get a new pushchair. On their return, the teacher asked how they had got on. The mum said she didn't know what to do as they had been offered a really heavy pushchair or a wheelchair and Imaan had immediately sat in the wheelchair announcing, 'I want this one.' The mum explained that she was worried about people staring at Imaan if she was in a wheelchair. She was reassured when the educator told her they had been having positive discussions about wheelchair users. When she realised that a wheelchair would stop people asking why a 4 year old was being pushed around in a pushchair, she decided to go for the wheelchair. She promised to give one of Imaan's old splints for a Doll to use.

Portraying both boy and girl Persona Dolls as powerful and non-stereo-typical can positively influence children's gender identity formation. It extends the range of interests, curiosity and aspirations of girls, while offering boys opportunities to express their feelings and develop con-centration. Challenging sexist comments and behaviour in a firm but sensitive, non-threatening way encourages children to suggest alter-native ways of thinking and doing. Persona Doll stories can encourage children to think about their attitudes and actions and suggest positive alternatives. To maximise their impact the Dolls need to be part of a curriculum that fosters gender equality and be used by people who understand and appreciate how important this is.

Feeling rejected

This story was told by a nursery school teacher to a group of children who had heard lots of happy and not so happy stories about their Persona Doll, Mohamed who is almost 4 years old. Their identification and bonding with him were already well-established.

> With Mohamed sitting on her knee, the teacher told the children that he was feeling upset and rejected. Having explained the concept, she drew their attention back to Mohamed by asking if they remembered him talking about a girl called Sophie. They nodded their affirmation and one of the children commented that Mohamed wants her to be his friend but that she doesn't want to be friends with him.

> After Mohamed had whispered in her ear, the teacher told the children what he had told her.

> Yesterday Sophie, June, Karen and Mandy were playing in the role-play area. Mohamed asked if he could play with them and Sophie said that he couldn't because he's a boy and they only play with girls.

> The children were asked to describe Mohamed's feelings. Their responses were empathetic, thoughtful and helpful. They talked about times when children hadn't wanted to play with them and how that had made them feel.

> When asked why they thought Sophie and her friends didn't want to play with boys, they offered a number of reasons and suggested possible solu-tions. The teacher used the Doll to counter their stereotypical comments and ended the story by feeding back the most appropriate responses: Mohamed says that Hugh is right. If Sophie doesn't want to play with him,

he should find someone else to be his friend. He says he felt so good when Megan told him that everyone here is his friend and he was so pleased when you all agreed with her.

Boys who enjoy traditional feminine activities may not be seen as 'real' boys and could be bullied – as the following story illustrates:

Meeting Sam

Close your eyes and when you open them you will see somebody you haven't met before. This is Sam. He lives with his sister Rose and their Mum in a small house. Sam is nearly 4 years old and Rose will soon be 6. They sleep in the same room in bunk beds. Who do you think sleeps at the top? Sam doesn't think that's fair but Rose says it is because she's the eldest.

Sam wants to know what you think.

[The children respond]

Sam says sometimes he likes sharing the room with Rose. When he's had a bad dream, he wakes up, it's dark, silent and creaky and he's really scared. Then he's really really glad that Rose is sleeping in the bunk above him. He's asked me to ask if any of you are scared of the dark.

[The children respond]

Sam loves it at playgroup. He wonders if you can guess what he and his best friend Sunita always do first thing in the morning? They dress up. Sam always puts on the long sparkly red dress and Sunita chooses the blue dress with white spots all over it. Sam puts on his favourite silver shoes with green bows and sometimes he wears a hat with three soft sticking-up pink feathers. Sunita wears the shiny pink shoes and the purple hat. They look at themselves in the long mirror and then go clop clop in their high-heeled shoes to do their next best thing: puzzles. They have to take off their dressing-up clothes when they paint or play outside.

There's something that Sunita can do that Sam wishes he could do. She speaks English like Sam does but she can also speak Urdu. Sam thinks that's terribly clever. Sunita is teaching him some Urdu songs and words. He wants to know if any of you can speak two languages like Sunita.

[The children respond]

On Sundays Sam and his sister Rose go to Sunday School with their uncle and aunty. Mum stays at home to cook. Sam says she's the best cook in the whole world. She gets lots of practice because she cooks lunch for the people who work in a big factory. Sam loves Sunday lunch especially when there's chicken, crispy roast potatoes, carrots and green peas. He's not so keen on fish, salad and cabbage. He wants to know if you have a special meal on Sundays and what you usually have?

[The children respond]

Sam has to go now. He says he's looking forward to coming to visit you again.

Sam's story

Last time Sam came to visit us, he was very happy. Do you remember that he went with his mum and Rose to the zoo? They had lots of fun: he loved the penguins best. How do you think Sam is feeling today? How can you tell?

[The children respond]

Would you like to know why he's feeling sad, miserable, fed-up and upset?

[The children respond]

It all started because his best friend Sunita wasn't at school yesterday. Do you remember what he always does with Sunita?

[The children respond]

Well yesterday he put on his favourite dress and shoes and was clop clopping along to the puzzle area. But he never got there. Ben and some of the other boys pointed their fingers at him and softly chanted so their teacher wouldn't hear:

'Look at Sam. He's a girl! He's a girl! We don't play with girls!!'

How do you think that made Sam feel?

[The children respond]

Sam asked me to ask you if any of you have ever been teased and laughed at? What happened? How did you feel?

[The children respond]

Sam's really worried that the same thing will happen tomorrow. If it does, what do you think he should do?

[Children respond]

Sam says you've given him lots of good ideas. He says thank you so much. He thinks telling his mum and his sister Rose will help to make him feel better: he's sure they'll give him big hugs. If he tells his teacher and she talks to Ben and his friends, that should stop the teasing and he's going to try and do what Susan suggested. He's going to ask his mum to ask Ben's mum if Ben can come to play so they can be friends. He says bye till next week.

A teacher was concerned that some of the boys were excluding girls from their games and verbally abusing them. At circle time she told the following Persona Doll story to highlight the pain that exclusion and verbal abuse brings and to deepen empathy with the victims. To avoid the children being recognised and to ensure that neither the Doll nor the story exactly mirrored the situation, she used a plump black boy Doll. While telling the story she constantly observed the girls whom she had seen being victimised in case they needed her support as well as the boys who had excluded and verbally abused them.

Empathising with Harry

The storytelling session began with the teacher asking the children if they remembered who was sitting on her lap. The response was immediate.

Having acknowledged their response the teacher passed Harry the Doll around the circle to give each child an opportunity to greet him individually. From the caring way they hugged and spoke to him they had obviously identified and bonded. Harry was their friend.

When asked about Harry's previous visit it was apparent from their replies that the story he had told impressed them and that they empathised with him. The question, 'Do you want to hear what happened to Harry at his nursery school on Friday?' was met with affirmative nods.

Harry told me that he was watching four boys building a garage with the bricks. When he tried to join in the biggest boy shouted at him

'You can't play here. We don't play with fatties.'

And the others yelled, 'Go way fatty, go way fatty.'

At this point the teacher maximised the children's input by giving them lots of opportunities to say what Harry was feeling, empathise with him and how they felt listening to his story. By asking questions like, 'How do you think that made Harry feel?' and 'Have you ever felt like that?' she encouraged them to talk about their own feelings and experiences. To extend their range of feeling words she asked them if they had ever been excluded and explained what the word meant.

These were some of their responses:

My brother always does that to me. He says, 'No girls!'

Julie used to be my friend but now she's best friends with Marie and Alice and they won't play with me.

My sister gets really upset when children in the park tease her because she doesn't walk properly.

My brother and his friends say I'm too small to play with them.

The children who have moved into the house next door told me they can't be friends with me 'cos they never play with brown children.

When my sister's friend comes to our house, the two of them run and hide away from me.

That's not fair.

The teacher agreed that it wasn't fair to exclude children, to make them feel sad and left out. She told them that Harry said he was so upset when those boys wouldn't let him play and called him names that he burst out crying. He said the boys laughed at him and said he was a cry baby. A discussion then ensued as to whether it was ok for boys to cry. The teacher drew their attention back to the story by asking them if it happened again what did they think Harry could do?

The children were eager to help Harry particularly as they considered he had been unfairly treated. They enjoyed offering him their advice and talking about their own experiences and actions. The teacher especially supported and picked up on the contributions of the girls who had been victims and of the boys who had excluded and abused them. She hoped that thinking about how Harry was feeling and empathising with him might have helped them gain insight into their own behaviour. She brought the story to an appropriate conclusion by weaving in the children's contributions, especially those that most closely matched the goal of the story.

Stories that reflect the Gypsy/Traveller children's lifestyle accurately and respectfully, acknowledge their fund of practical knowledge and first-hand experience of, for example, plants, animals and the geography of the country are told whether or not there are Gypsy/Traveller children in the group. Because they develop empathy and close bonding, Persona Dolls can encourage children to revisit and reflect on their prejudiced attitudes and appreciate that even if their life-style is different from the Doll's, they share many experiences and feelings:

Meeting Bridget

Bridget is 4 years old. She is wearing her best dress today. Usually she only wears it for church but her mum said she could put it on today to come and visit you all. There are lots of people in her family. She has a mum and a dad, a big brother, a big sister and twin baby girls. They live in two trailers on a site with lots of other families who also live in trailers. A trailer is a home on wheels. They used to live in one trailer but after the twins were born they got another one. Bridget really likes her new trailer because it is much bigger than the old one and she has her own room. Her favourite thing is riding her purple bike around the site. Her dad took off the stabilisers last week. Bridget thinks that she's probably the fastest girl on the site, maybe in the whole of Manchester! She would like to know if you are also good bike riders.

(The children respond)

Bridget and her family have been living on this site for about six months. It is near the park and her new school. She says she likes her teacher and she's got a special playground buddy who helps out if she doesn't have anyone to play with. At her last school people used to call her and her family horrible names. She has bad dreams sometimes about when people used to be nasty to her in the playground. She wonders if you have bad dreams.

(The children respond)

Bridget and her family are travelling back to Ireland in the summer holidays. She's really looking forward to it because her grannies and grandpas, aunts, uncles and her fifteen cousins will be there! Bridget loves being with all of them. She says she'd really like to know what you're going to do in the holidays.

(The children respond)

Working with students

Sally Elton-Chalcraft, a lecturer at St Martin's College in Lancaster, explains how and why she uses the Persona Doll approach with her students. She hopes that the hands-on role-playing experience will help them to appreciate the power of the Dolls and how to work with them in the classroom. To extend their learning and to encourage them to think critically about the approach and the part that the Dolls can play in primary Religious Education, she asks them to answer the following questions:

- How effective are Persona Dolls in encouraging children to learn about and learn from Religion?

■ How could you use a Doll to teach about the Sikh festival of Baisakhi?

■ How could you use a Doll to teach about the Christian festival of Christmas and the Muslim festival of Eid-Ul-Fitr?

■ What are the advantages and limitations of using a Persona Doll in RE?

The role-play – introducing Jeetinder

The students sat in a circle and the lecturer held the Persona Doll on her knee. She began by talking about the role of the teacher as facilitator and mediator and then modelled a lesson by role-playing being a class teacher. The student teachers and trainees role-played being the children in the class. In the first session which was a getting to know you session, the Sikh Persona Doll told the children about himself. They engaged with the Doll, responded to the questions the 'teacher' posed and asked their own.

The 'teacher' starts by telling the 'children' that this is Jeetinder Singh, he is aged 8 and in Year 3 at school. He would like to know some of your names.

A few of the 'children' tell him their name.

On his way to visit us, Jeetinder told me he went on the slide and swings in the park. The slide is his favourite and he wonders what yours are?

The 'children' share their preferences

[Doll whispers in the teacher's ear]

Jeetinder wants me to tell you about his family. His grandparents came to Britain from the Punjab in 1970 when Jeetinder's Dad was 10 years old. (Show children where the Punjab is on the map.) Jeetinder lives with his Mum and Dad and his 14 year old sister Manjit and his 11 year old brother Tejpreet. They go to secondary school and on Sundays they both go to Punjabi school. Jeetinder says that when he's a bit older he's going to go with them. Everybody in his family speaks Punjabi and English.

Jeetinder says his favourite food is vegetable curry and dhal which is made from lentils. He also likes fish and chips, especially from the chip shop round the corner from his house. He wants to know what your favourite foods are.

The 'children' talk about their favourite foods and why they like them so much?

[Doll whispers in teacher's ear]

In the mornings Jeetinder says he gets up, has a wash, eats breakfast and gets ready for school. His mum helps him tie his *Jurra*, his top knot (the children may have already asked about it). Jeetinder says that his family are Sikhs and in the Sikh religion they believe it is important to keep their hair long. He has long hair tied up in his *Jurra* and so does his brother, Tejpreet. His dad's hair is so long that he wears it in a turban. Jeetinder says it takes him quite a while to put it on. Jeetinder's cousin Jagdeep doesn't wear a *Jurra* and his dad, Jeetinder's uncle, doesn't wear a turban because they have short hair but they are still Sikhs!

[Doll whispers in teacher's ear]

Jeetinder is the only Sikh in the juniors and he sometimes gets teased by children in Year 5 and 6 because of his *Jurra*. He wants to know if any of you have been teased about your hair? What did it feel like? What did you do? He wants to know what you think he can do.

The 'children' offer various suggestions.

The students learned that the point of this session is for the children to see Jeetinder as a child just like them who likes playing in parks, gets up in the morning and washes and gets ready for school, likes chips but Jeetinder is a Sikh who takes his religion very seriously. Emphasis is placed on the diversity within Sikhism. For example Jagdeep's family's beliefs are different from those of Jeetinder's.

The Naming Ceremony for Jeetinder's cousin

The lecturer once again takes the role of the teacher, with Jeetinder on her knee and the students role-play being the children.

Jeetinder whispers in the teacher's ear and she tells the 'children' that last Sunday his cousin Amanpreet's baby sister was named at the Gurdwara (temple). He said Amanpreet had a smile which filled up the whole of her face and that her Mum, Aneet Kaur and her Dad, Raminder were very proud. Amanpreet wore a lovely new green shalwar kamize. (The 'children' were asked if they knew what these were: special tunic and trousers.) Jeetinder, his brother and his sister had new clothes for the ceremony.

[Doll whispers in teacher's ear]

Jeetinder wonders what clothes you wear on special occasions.

Some of the children described their traditional clothes while others talked about their best ones.

[Doll whispers in teacher's ear]

Jeetinder said it was very exciting because everyone crowded into the Gurdwara. When the Guru Granth Sahib (the holy book) was opened, they all held their breath in anticipation as whispered rumours spread through the hall that the first letter of the baby's name was to begin with A. The same letter as her sister! Sometimes at naming ceremonies parents can't think of a name straight away so they go away and decide later but Amanpreet's new sister was called Amritpal at once. Everybody sang songs and Jeetinder prayed that Amritpal would grow up to be a good friend to him and Amanpreet. He says he's looking forward to when she's two years old because that's when little ones get interesting. He doesn't like them when they're babies because they have poohy nappies and are sick!

[Doll whispers in teacher's ear]

Jeetinder told me that they had a big party with lots of food. He asks if you have parties when your babies are named.

The students then talked about different naming ceremonies.

4

Persona Dolls and the primary curriculum

I t says something about the Persona Doll approach that boys and girls at key stage 1 and 2 can willingly suspend belief, engage and identify with the Dolls and seriously offer them advice and support. The fact that they bond so readily is one of the reasons why the Dolls are such powerful learning tools. Not only do they make a valuable contribution to the learning and teaching of PSHCE, Citizenship and Religious Education – the areas that spring most readily to mind – but also to Literacy and History and across the curriculum. Children who have heard a good many Persona Doll stories are likely to demonstrate that they can think critically and independently and are able to express their opinions confidently while actively listening to other views.

Case Study

This school values and appreciates its Persona Dolls

Aboyne Lodge School in St Albans places great emphasis on the personal, social and emotional development of the children. As part of their holistic approach to this work staff use Persona Dolls. Headteacher Linda Crawley describes how working with the Dolls developed in the school and how the Persona Doll approach has, in turn, influenced other areas of work.

When I took over the school about five years ago, it was a good school and one of our development priorities was to do something about PSHCE, ethos and behavior. My leadership team was debating how to do this and someone mentioned Persona Dolls and we thought this might be it. Because we were a Beacon School we had extra money for collaborating with other schools and were able to organise a day conference on Persona Dolls at a hotel that offered good food. We bought a full set of Dolls to represent a range of cultures and additional needs.

Back at school, we decided to give a Doll to every class and that the children would make up the personas. We very quickly discovered that you just can't do that with years 4, 5 and 6 because there was definite resistance and cynicism – well, it's just a doll – and the staff did not feel it would work with this age group. We tried it for about half a term and then decided to do what we have done successfully with everything else, to introduce them from the bottom up at the foundation stage where there is still magic and the children would not think of them as dolls, but as friends. And that's what's happened. The children really do believe in them. I remember a Year 1 class who'd just moved from Reception. The teacher was using the Doll to 'talk' about her camping holiday. All the children went off to write about their holidays and the Doll was left on the teacher's chair. She noticed that one little boy went over and was whispering to it so she asked him what he was saying. He replied that he was just asking her what colour the tent was!

The Dolls are kept in the teachers' cupboards and brought out when teachers feel they need to use them at circle time. They are not used by everyone,or all the time, but they are used consistently to cover a whole lot of issues. At the end of the year the children move classes with their Doll. As new things happen or new problems arise, they are discussed and written down and kept with the Doll in a big book bag so that the next class teacher knows what's happened: knows the Dolls name, brothers and sisters and what has happened during the year: all the details are there. Just as there is a handover for the children, there is also a handover for the Doll.

The children all do Philosophy which provides another opportunity to discuss issues in a theoretical way. Previous discussions around the Dolls help because they enable the children to empathise and think about other people's points of view.

I think that because of our buddy system and because of the Dolls, the atmosphere in the school is quite different – there are no two ways about it: you just walk into the school and the children are so lovely and kind to each other. I know that headteachers sing the praises of their own schools, but everyone has remarked on it. We hardly ever have any problems in the playground: I'm not saying we don't have arguments, because we do, but we have trained up peer mediators to help children sort out their own problems.

A lot of this development stemmed from looking at how the Dolls worked and how we could extend the understandings that were being developed. We have introduced SEAL (part of the primary strategy: social and emotional aspects of learning) which is an absolutely superb programme and the Dolls are used with it.

The Dolls have helped me as a head to encourage staff develop positive attitudes to difference and to tackle discrimination confidently. I think the teachers here would say that they feel less worried.

LITERACY AND PSHCE

This Literacy Hour was skilfully and successfully built around a Persona Doll from a Sikh family called Gurgit, whom the children in Year 1 had met several times and with whom they had bonded and identified. The Doll provided a focus for the lesson and enabled the teacher to raise an important issue in a non-threatening and stimulating way. The children were told that one of Gurjit's favourite things was going to Karate club. On his way home one day he looked in his bag and found a nasty letter. He brought it in to show them. Each working with a partner, they enthusiastically worked out what it said. This is a copy of the letter:

> Gurgit
>
> We don't want you coming
>
> to our karate club anymore.
>
> Stay away from here paki.
>
> We don't like pakis.
>
> Get the message or
>
> we'll bash you up.

In the ensuing discussion the children empathised with Gurgit. One of the girls said: 'It hurts your heart – it doesn't matter what colour you are'. With great effort and concentration each child wrote a sentence about what had happened to Gurgit. When they were asked what they thought should happen next, a little boy sensibly suggested: 'The Karate man should tell the boys that they couldn't come to Karate club anymore but that Gurgit could'. The ideas they expressed and the way they identified and empathised with Gurgit's feelings suggest that this was not only a stimulating literacy experience but also a social and emotional one.

A school in north west London has two Persona Dolls, Samira and Isaac. The teacher of this Year 3 class uses the Dolls to develop the children's literacy skills through making books about the Dolls, writing letters to them, writing about them and drawing pictures of them. They made and sent cards to Samira on her birthday. The fact that she came from Bangladesh aroused their interest so they looked at a map to see where it was, talked about the religion, the languages Samira and her family speak, the food Samira ate when she lived in Bangladesh and whether she eats the same food in London . Most of the children had never heard of Bangladesh.

The teacher also uses the Dolls to encourage children to talk about their anxieties. She told a story about Samira who was finding maths really difficult and one of the children responded, 'I feel like that' and later remarked, 'Samira's feeling all scared that she's going to get her maths all wrong.' The teacher used a Doll with her previous year group because a few children were not confident with literacy. They responded to the story by admitting that, 'their tummies also felt funny'.

> Samara came and she told us loads of things about her friends and family. I told her how to walk away from mean people. We talked about when we were all new at School and how to make friends. I hope She comes again and brings her brother Issac. I want to see her again to tell her I like her, and its fun when she comes to circle time.

Samera shared her problems with me and I would tell her things, is she comes again.

Samera

Marna

Whene Semire came to are class room she told us about her game coaled James bond. She wass having

some Problems about that exact game because thay she fourt thay where

catching her and ganging up on her. She came because she was having Problems about her relashonships. because we were having Problems with are relashonships and she made us feel more happier. because she teached us not to run and lock ourselves in the toilet if some one was ganging up on you but tell the teacher and sort it out Properly.

BY Alisa age 8 year 3

52

During Anti-Bullying Week an educator in Swindon told her Y6 class a story about Holly their Persona Doll. She has a best friend called Julia: they have been friends ever since they first started school together. It's going to be Julia's birthday next week and she hasn't invited Holly, although other girls in the class have been invited. Holly can't remember doing or saying anything to upset Julia but feels she must have done something wrong. She hasn't told her mum yet. She doesn't know what to say. The two families always do things together, even going on holiday.

What should Holly do? She doesn't want to cause a problem but doesn't understand what's going on. The teacher asks the children to help Holly by doing the following:

- take a few minutes to talk to the person on either side of you about Holly's problem

- make a few notes about what she could do

- what advice have you got for Holly?

- how are the other girls feeling who will be going to the party?

- what reason could there be for not inviting Holly?

- what more information do you need to help you find a solution to the problem?

- does Holly's school or class have rules to help avoid people being left out?

- if they don't have any could you make some?

When she spoke to us she made me think how I play with my friends and how I must look after their feelings.

by Emma Warner age 7 year three

HISTORY

Part of the history curriculum is about children's own lives and that of their parents and community. A Doll that the children have never met before could come into the classroom as someone who is living through some particular incident in the past (but the children are there with it, also travelling through time). This becomes an interesting way for children to see the world through the eyes of someone in the past.

Another possibility is to use the Dolls as a second stage in working on historical or citizenship issues. The children might be learning about people in the Civil Rights movement in the States. A Black Persona Doll visits and talks about how he or she is finding it hard to get treated respectfully and fairly today.

As part of their study of Britain since the 30s, the children might read *Candle in the Dark*, in which Clara and Maxi come on the Kindertransport and settle with an English family (Geras, 2005). A Persona Doll the children have never seen before, Clara or Maxi, could come to the classroom. The children could be encouraged to ask previously prepared questions and respond appropriately to the questions and ideas the Doll offers.

By celebrating social justice festivals children learn about how people's struggles in the past have helped to create a better life for themselves and others. Stories about the history of resistance also challenge the myth that Black people, women and people with disabilities were or are passive victims. Stories woven around the lives of people who have played a part in the struggle for human rights can inspire children and deepen their understanding of and commitment to combating injustice. The children may have parents and grandparents who actively participated or still participate in trade union activities or liberation struggles or who remember discriminatory incidents from their childhood. They could be invited to come and tell their stories. Although these stories would not be woven around the Dolls, the Dolls could listen and contribute stories about members of their families of whom they are proud.

When celebrating the anniversary of the abolition of the Atlantic slave trade on March 25th with older children, a Black Doll could tell them a story about somebody in its family who ran away from a plantation a very long long time ago because it was so badly treated. Berenice Miles (2006) stresses that children need to understand that thousands of slaves took part in uprisings that greatly contributed to the eventual ending of the slave trade and that thousands of British women and men actively supported the campaign against slavery. Women's Day on March 8th offers children, educators and parents an opportunity to honour the women they know, as well as famous women they might not know about, such as Harriet Tubman.

CITIZENSHIP EDUCATION

Key stage 1 and 2 pupils are expected to learn about themselves as developing individuals and as members of their communities. Anti-discriminatory education and the promotion of citizenship are intrinsically linked and both necessitate:

- empowering children to talk confidently about their experiences and feelings

- supporting their sense of identity and belonging

- developing their understanding of fairness and unfairness

- boosting their ability to empathise

- helping them understand how racism and other inequalities affect their lives and the lives of their peers

Active citizenship education encourages children to be enthusiastic and critical learners. Opportunities are provided for children to learn about people who are ethnically and culturally similar to and different from them. They are given the skills they need to challenge unfairness and stand up for what they believe is right. 'It's not fair!' is a familiar cry, proclaimed with feeling. With encouragement, guidance and support children can develop strategies and confidence to deal with unfair situations and to realise that they can bring about change. Through Persona Doll stories, educators can address superior patronising attitudes and encourage and support those who express egalitarian ideas.

Information is communicated in a relaxed and friendly way and any inaccurate ideas are challenged. Educators can tell stories that give correct information and encourage the children to think about their ideas and attitudes. This can also help them realise that sometimes what they have been told is untrue:

Joe has a problem

When the children in Year 1 came in from break, they were pleased to see Joe waiting to tell them a story. The teacher told them that he needed their help. He was confused and didn't know what was true and what wasn't. The children were very willing to try and help him.

Joe had asked his Nan why his friend Thandi's skin is brown and his isn't. She told him it is because Thandi was born in a very hot country far far away and she got burnt by the sun and that Joe was born in Manchester so that's why his skin is pinkish. But when Joe told Thandi what his Nan had said, she shook her head. She'd never ever lived in a very hot country. She didn't think that her mum and dad, her grandma and grandpa, her aunts and uncles or her cousins had ever lived in one either *and* she too was born in Manchester. Joe had brought a picture of Thandi to show the teacher and the children and this was passed around the circle.

The teacher asked the children why they thought Thandi's skin was brown. They made various suggestions. She picked up on any misinformation and went on to explain that they all had something called melanin in their skin which they couldn't see but which was definitely there. They would know if they had a lot because their skin would be dark like Thandi's and if they had a little, their skin would be light like Joe's. She asked the children, while helping Joe, to put their hands palms down on their laps and to look at the colour of their skin. They decided who had the most melanin and who had the least. Joe was sat on a chair and the children lined up: those with the darkest skin in the front and those with the lightest at the back.

The teacher helped the children at each table to make a chart illustrating what they had found out and the children drew pictures of themselves and coloured them it to show how much melanin they thought they had in their skins. While doing this, one of the children said that when she went to the outdoor swimming pool, her mum made her put sun cream on all over so the sun couldn't burn her skin. This remark triggered a chorus of similar experiences and a lively exchange of information about the harmful effect the sun's rays could have if they didn't pro-tect themselves. The children were surprised to learn from Joe that when his family and Thandi's went to the seaside, his mum and Thandi's mum insisted on both children having sun cream all over them.

At the end of the session the Doll whispered in the teacher's ear. She told the children that Joe said he was so glad he'd talked to them about his problem and that he couldn't wait to tell his Nan about melanin!

A teacher in a school in Peterborough wanted to create an authentic persona for a Polish Doll because some of the parents were experiencing prejudice and antagonism.

As she had little in-depth knowledge she decided to interview the parents of the Polish children in her class. From the various responses she created this persona:

Beata, aged 8, lives in a small modern house with an even smaller garden with her mum Olga, dad Lech and one year old brother Janek. She shares a room with Janek. Beata has no pets but would love a dog like she had when she lived in Poland. It was big brown and furry. But in those days they didn't live in a town like Peterborough, their home was in a village so there was lots of space for dogs to run around in. Beata's grandparents still live there. She visits them in the summer holidays.

Beata calls her parents, Mama and Tata. Dad is a carpenter. He came to work here first and after about a year Beata and her mum came. Janek was born here. Mum was a teacher in Poland but now works at home cleaning, cooking, doing the washing and looking after Janek and Beata. The family speak Polish at home.

Beata goes to Polish school on Saturdays where she reads, writes, does art and craft and learns about Polish history and geography. She feels very proud to be Polish. She and her dad both speak English better than mum does. Beata finds writing in English quite difficult. Beata's family are Roman Catholic and they attend the Polish church. Beata's favourite Polish festivals are Children's Day on the first of June because she and Janek get presents and mum cooks a special dinner and St Nicholas Day on the 6th of December because her grandparents come to visit. St Nicholas, dressed like a bishop, comes at night and hides small presents in the bedroom of good children. If they have been naughty he leaves a stick! Beata makes sure she's very good.

Beata likes her new school, especially her teacher, doing maths and playing with her friends but she doesn't like the wind, rain and all the cars and people in Peterborough. What she likes best about Poland are her grandparents and playing in the forest near their house with friends, building snow castles and sliding on the ice in winter. In Peterborough she enjoys playing with her Barbie doll, drawing and painting, watching TV and going to the cinema. She doesn't like barking dogs or Janek crying and waking her up at night.

Her favourite foods are chicken, chips, tuna sandwiches, goilabki (a polish dish of cabbage leaves stuffed with mince, rice and carrot in tomato sauce) beetroot soup, chicken soup with noodles, and polish stew of cabbage meat and tomato sauce. She doesn't like fish, baked potatoes, Polish bread and school dinners.

The teacher also asked the parents for realistic incidents that could be developed into Persona Doll stories. This is what they suggested:

- what's in a name? The children tell Beata that her name is funny and they're going to call her Bee. When they see her in the playground, they flap their 'wings' and make buzzing noises. She's feeling angry and upset and wants to know what she can do

- an unfriendly act: A horribly smelly bin bag has been emptied all over the neighbour's doorstep. Beata says they also come from Poland and they're very nice. She can't understand why anybody would want to do such an unkind thing. She wonders if the children have any ideas

- Polish food: Beata takes a packed lunch to school. One of the children pulls a face and says, 'That's yucky, that is, and smelly. I wouldn't eat it if you paid me!' She asks the children how they think that made her feel and what they would have done if they heard and saw what happened?

Refugee children who are coping with losing their parents, siblings, members of their extended family and friends as well as losing their home, favourite toys and pets may get support and security from the Dolls and simple stories that deal with loss. Drawing on children's past personal experience requires appropriate professional judgement and sensitivity. Some children might feel uncomfortable if required to draw on recent traumatic events.

Using a refugee Persona Doll with whom the children have identified and bonded may help to reduce the impact of the negative images and stories non-refugee children are exposed to. Stories provide valuable opportunities for children from refugee and asylum seeking families to develop their self-confidence and self-esteem.

To help children empathise with the plight of refugee and asylum seeker families, the Portsmouth Ethnic Minority Achievement Service used the Dolls with Year 1 and Year 2 children. This example is of a teacher introducing a Doll that the children were meeting for the first time. The Doll's persona, the reasons for leaving Iran and the dangerous journey to the UK to seek asylum were based on stories in the media and on people's real experiences. To add realism and stimulate interest, photographs were found on the internet and culturally relevant artefacts such as clothing were obtained from friends. The photo album provided a visual focus for discussion around people, places and events. The educator emphasised the experiences that the Doll shared with the other 5 year old children and used opportunities to celebrate similarities and differences.

With the Doll sitting on her lap, the teacher began the introduction.

Meeting Sibel

This is Sibel. She is 5 years old, she'll soon be 6. She lives with her mum and dad, her big sister Sara and her little brother Talan James who was born in England. The rest of her family live a long way away in Iran: she misses them very much. Sibel speaks Kurdish at home: she can speak quite a lot of English now. Her Daddy speaks English very well and her mummy has learned some English at her classes. Sibel and her family live in a flat now; they've just moved into it and like it very much because it is their first real home in England. At last they've got their own front door. It's blue. Sibel sleeps in a big bed that she shares with her sister: they like sleeping together in their big bed better than being in their own beds.

She enjoys going to the beach, the park and the library. She also likes drawing, going to places with her family, playing school with her sister, putting on her special clothes and looking at her photos. She likes her mummy's cooking, especially the sweet sticky cakes and she likes cucumber, red pepper, chicken, popcorn and chips and ice-cream.

She doesn't like going on buses and she doesn't like doors being shut. She doesn't like sausages or fish or baked beans. She worries about getting lost, being away from her family, and starting school.

The children were encouraged to think and talk about things like leaving home, friends and family, who they would miss most if they had to leave suddenly, having to choose a favourite thing to take away with them, what it might be like starting school for the first time in another country where no-one spoke their language and how they would help someone to settle in to their class who was not able to speak much English. They came up with all the right supportive strategies.

The session ended with the children saying goodbye to Sibel.

School and class councils promote citizenship

Citizenship education and school and class councils provide children with opportunities to gain the knowledge, understanding and skills they need to play an effective role as informed, thoughtful and responsible individuals aware of their rights and responsibilities. Being involved in the electoral process, being members of the school and class councils and participating in the consultation process gives all pupils opportunities to become actively involved in decision making and power-sharing. Their voices are heard, listened to and their decisions acted upon. These are empowering procedures.

The following example describes how a local authority in the Midlands piloted the use of a Persona Doll to spark children's interest in and knowledge about the school council. It was hoped that their responses to the Doll would give the team a clearer idea of their understanding of their roles and responsibilities:

- adults would be able to feed in ideas through the Doll whilst keeping it child-orientated and not perceived as adult led

- children would share ideas and express their concerns. Children new to year 1 would have the opportunity to learn about the basic organisation and expectations associated with the school council.

The Doll John, was introduced briefly to the group of twelve Year 1 and Year 2 children who had met many Persona Dolls before. So they knew John wasn't a pupil at their school but just visiting. They were told that he had moved to a new school that has a school council. There wasn't one at his old school so he didn't know what it was for or anything else about it. He then 'asked' the children questions about their council. One of the team wrote down the children's responses:

- it meets on Wednesdays, after lunch in the library

- there is a sign on the door to say they are meeting

- they have to remember to go to the meeting without their teachers telling them – they remind each other in the playground on Tuesdays

- there's elections and we all vote

- if you win then you can be on the council

■ at meetings they talk about all sorts of things and we get a chance to say if we agree

■ teachers make most of the rules but people on the Council make some

■ they try to make the school a better place.

Following this question and answer session the children took it in turns to hold John, tell him their name and chat to him. Everyone participated and nobody ever made comments like, 'it's only a Doll' during the session. The children asked if John could visit again soon. Photos of John and the children were taken and an account of the visit written up.

The team agreed that using the Dolls in this way met their expectations. Many schools have adapted this model and incorporated it into their citizenship programme. Persona Doll stories like the following can be used to spark discussion about elections and in the process provide information, discover what the children know and arouse their interest:

Meg's story

Meg hasn't been to see us for a very long time so in case you've forgotten what she told us about herself and her family, I'll remind you. She's nearly 9 years old. Her mum Tracey works in a huge factory and her dad Mark is a long-distance lorry driver. You remember Meg said she wished he worked in a shop around the corner because then he wouldn't be away such a lot. William is Meg's baby brother. She told us that he can't walk or talk properly and is cute but he cries a lot and he often stinks!!! Their grandma looks after them when mum and dad are at work. Meg's got her own bedroom but William sleeps in grandma's room.

Meg spends most days reading and playing football with her cousin Jamie and her friends. She practices a lot and hopes that one day she'll be in her school team.

[Doll whispers in teacher's ear]

Meg says that at Jamie's school the boys don't let the girls play football. She wants to know what you think about that. She says please don't all shout at once or you'll give her a headache.

[The children respond]

[Doll whispers in teacher's ear]

Meg asks if you remember when she visited ages ago, you told her about your school council and she said she wished there was one in her school? Well, her wish has come true! The bad news is that when her teacher explained to the class about the election, Meg says she was ill in bed so she doesn't know much about it. She remembers that you told her that you all voted for somebody from your class to be a member of the council but she can't remember anything else. She wants to know if lots of people in your class wanted to be on the council?

[The children respond]

[Doll whispers in teacher's ear]

Meg says she really really wants to be the person from her class that gets elected to their new school council but she's not sure how to go about it. When you had elections, she wonders how you decided who would be the best person to vote for.

[The children respond]

[Doll whispers in teacher's ear]

Meg asks what you think she should do and say to get children in her class to vote for her.

[The children make some suggestions]

[Doll whispers in teacher's ear]

Meg says thank you so much. You've given her lots of good ideas and practical suggestions that she thinks there's a good chance that by the time she visits again, she'll be a member of her school council!

Addressing topical issues

The QCA requires that children are given opportunities to consider social and moral dilemmas they might encounter related to aggression and violence, questions of fairness, the right and wrong way to behave and political issues. Through the Persona Doll stories they tell, educators meet these QCA requirements. At the same time they also respond to any superior or patronising attitudes children express and encourage and support those who put forward egalitarian ideas.

World events shown on TV expose children to many images of war and conflict. Racist outpourings and physical attacks followed 9/11 and the bombings in London on 7/7. The tabloids particularly targeted Muslims but Sikhs also suffered the consequences. An article in the *Guardian* (September 5 2005) headed 'Mistaken identity' reported that :

> ... Dal Singh Dhesy, a worker with the Sikh community and youth centre in Handsworth, Birmingham, thinks that Sikhs have had a worse time of it than Muslims – because of their turbans. There is a grim irony to this: turbans are a potent symbol of Sikh identity, but, somehow, certain sections of the white population have come to (wrongly) associate them with Islamist extremists. Dal says he experiences name-calling and stares from White people on a daily basis, and describes other Sikhs who face physical attack and intimidation.

The stories told through the Dolls can help counter the stream of Islamophobic views and attitudes expressed on television and in the press, especially the tabloids. Children have many opportunities to see and hear them: at home, in the playground, visiting friends and relations. These comments are usually negative.

In the following example a Persona Doll is being used respectfully, sensitively and empathetically in a Year 5 class of children who are all White.

Davinder's story

It is circle time and Davinder, a Sikh Doll, is sitting on the teacher's knee with her face buried in his chest. She is a frequent visitor.

The teacher begins the session by asking:

Who is sitting on my lap?

The response is instantaneous. She then asks 'and what is Davinder wearing?' There is a a short pause before a chorus volunteers: 'her *salwar kamize*'.

How do you think she's feeling today?

[The children respond and the teacher agrees. 'You're right. She is feeling sad, upset and miserable. Would you like to know why?'

Nods of agreement.

Doll whispers in teacher's ear.

> Davinder told me that it's because something really awful happened to her dad when he came home from work last week. He got off the bus like he usually does. He walked along the pavement as he usually does. He saw a

group of men laughing and shouting on the other side of the road. He took no notice of them: he thought they were just messing about. But then they crossed the road, rushed up to him and made a small circle around him so he couldn't walk away from them.

How do you think Davinder's dad felt?

[The children respond]

Doll whispers in teacher's ear

Yes. He was frightened, worried, surprised and angry.

Davinder says they then called him horrible names but her dad wouldn't tell her what they were. She says she's never been called horrid names and wants to know if you've ever been. How did you feel?

[The children respond]

Doll whispers in teacher's ear.

Davinder says they called her dad a murderer! They said he'd instructed those people to plant the bombs on the tube trains and on the London bus that killed all those people. She wants to know if you saw those pictures on TV.

[The children respond]

Doll whispers in teacher's ear.

Davinder asked me to remind you that her family are vegetarians because they believe that it's wrong to kill and eat animals or fish. She says her dad doesn't even kill a fly or a mosquito buzzing round him. He certainly wouldn't be involved in the killing of people. When they saw the aeroplane crashing into the building on TV, Davinder says her mum and dad were shocked, upset and angry. She says they were so upset they didn't even help her with her homework or read to her as they usually did. She says there's no way her dad could have had anything to do with that bombing.

Doll whispers in teacher's ear.

Davinder says the men then shouted at her dad, 'Go back to Pakistan'. She says her dad and mum and all the family were born in London and none of them have ever been to Pakistan.

One of the men then did something shocking. He pulled off Davinder's dad's turban, threw it on the ground and trampled all over it! Luckily at that moment some cars stopped, people jumped out and the men ran away.

> Davinder says her dad is feeling much better now. But there's something worrying her and she wonders if you can help. She really can't work out why those men thought her dad could have had anything to do with those bombs and why they picked on him and treated him so badly? She wants to know what you think?

[The children respond]

Doll whispers in teacher's ear.

> Davinder says she's really pleased that she's told you about what happened to her dad because it's made her feel a bit better talking about it. She's going to sit on the special chair so you can cuddle and talk to her if you want to.

THE CREATIVE CURRICULUM

A project on journeys that involved PSHCE, Citizenship, Literacy skills, Arts and Crafts and History was developed by a Year 4 teacher. The children shared their experiences of holiday trips and as there were no children from refugee or asylum-seeking families in the class, Philani, a Persona Doll was included to deepen children's understanding of what it means to have to leave home, family, friends and everything that is familiar and precious. Philani was used throughout the project, sometimes sharing his experiences with the children, sometimes simply listening and sometimes initiating discussion.

The two Gypsy/Traveller children in the class were encouraged and supported so they felt comfortable about sharing their experiences. To ensure that she had a good idea of their day to day lives, the teacher had visited the site where they lived several times and had spent time with the parents. She was told about the trauma one of the families had been through. Police had forced them to leave a site where they had lived for nearly three years and then they had had a long and stressful time before finding this one.

The teacher introduced Philani to the children by telling them a few important things about his persona. Over the weeks and through the stories he 'told' they learnt about why and how he and his parents left Zimbabwe and how they eventually arrived in Britain. They empathised with him especially when Philani told them that his mum and dad were waiting anxiously to hear whether they would be given permission to stay in this country. They didn't know what they would do if permission was refused. Returning to Zimbabwe wasn't an option. The teacher initiated the first of many discussions about what it was like being a refugee and encouraged the Gypsy/Traveller children to talk about what they liked about living in a trailer and gave them opportunities to talk if they wanted to about negatives aspects: like the shortage of sites and being harassed.

On one of his visits, the teacher asked Philani if he had any pictures of his house and the friends and relations he had left behind in Zimbabwe. He said he had a few and would love to show the class. When he brought them in, the teacher explained that they were pictures of the people and things he missed most and so were very precious to him. The house he used to live in, his grandma and grandpa, his best friend, his cat, his dog and his bicycle. Philani was asked if he would like the pictures to be passed around. He agreed as long as the children handled them carefully.

The teacher then told them about a great idea Philani had told her about. He was going to put his pictures in a book and write about each one and, because it was such a special book, he was going to make the cover look really cool. He didn't have photos of everything or everyone so he was going to draw things like the park where he and his friends played football and the tree they used to love climbing and sitting in. He asked the children if they liked his idea and if they wanted to copy it. The teacher and the rest of the class thought it was a great idea and over the next few weeks, they become very involved in and proud of their books.

On one of his visits Philani whispered in the teacher's ear that he had written a poem about being a refugee and that he was going to put it in his book. The teacher asked if she could read it to the class and Philani said she could.

PHILANI'S POEM
Imagine soldiers come to your house
you have to hide,
Imagine crouched in a small cupboard
Scared, terrified.
Imagine walking, running, leaving,
Screaming.
Imagine having to leave your home,
Imagine being all alone

Hearing Philani's poem inspired some of the children to write a poem to put in their books. Their poems expressed their compassion, empathy and understanding of what being a refugee might be like:

WHEN

When they chase you out of your house
  and you don't know where to go.
When you live in the wild and see death
   all around you.
When you climb over sharp rocks
  mountains and cliffs.
When you go to sleep crying and wake up
    sad.
When you walk forever and it seems you don't get
   anywhere.
When you get across the border and have to
  live in a place where they don't speak your language.
When all around you are people who don't
    care about you for they don't know what
     you've been through.

A REFUGEE'S EXPERIENCE

What if you were running through a
battlefield where it was raining with
shells, bullets exploding behind you,
screams of death and the constant
chatter of the guns, with rubble
falling down everywhere?
what will happen at the border?
will you get past or be pushed in
the dust told to return to where
you came from?
Imagine living a life of fear.

To reinforce and follow up on book-making and the theme of the project, journeys, the teacher read *Journey to Jo'burg* (Naidoo, 2008) to Philani and the children. Group discussions encouraged the children to express their feelings and opinions about the story and the characters. Philani's 'questions' and 'comments' were used to spark reflection and debate. A visit by Beverley Naidoo thrilled and excited the children, deepening their understanding and involvement with the characters and the story and giving them a glimpse of what life was like in apartheid South Africa.

PROMOTING REFLECTION AND CRITICAL THINKING

Educators extend the ideas, opinions and feelings shared during SEAL and Persona Doll storytelling sessions, especially those that raise issues and pose dilemmas and problems. To actively participate in these discussions and group activities, children need to have a wide vocabulary, the ability to think critically and logically and to express their ideas clearly. It is remarkable how much misinformation children have in their heads: erroneous ideas and stereotypical views. Tasks like the following can help to develop these skills and continue the process of unlearning and rethinking:

What do you think?

Is it true that only girls are frightened of spiders? How do you know?
Is it true that all bus drivers are men? How do you know?
Is it true that women are good at fixing things? How do you know?
Is it ok for boys to cry when they are hurt? How do you know?
Is it true that all children live in houses with their parents? How do you know?
Does everybody eat meat? How do you know?

Moving

Encourage the children to talk about their experiences of moving from one class to another, from one home to another, to another town, from one part of the country to another, from one country to another. Be particularly sensitive to refugee and Gypsy/Traveller children, who may have had traumatic experiences. If appropriate, encourage them to talk about this and to express their feelings.

Discuss the different ways in which people move their bodies: walking, running, crawling, waving, nodding, stamping. Encourage them to move in various ways to music, choosing music from a range of cultures, including Gypsy/Travellers'.

Encourage the children to talk about all the different forms of transport that help people move from place to place. Then ask them to draw some of them. Ensure that trailers, caravans, wheelchairs and walking frames are included.

I'm special

Provide mirrors, large pieces of paper, a range of skin colour crayons and pencils, materials of different sizes, shapes, colours and textures and strong glue and encourage the children to draw themselves and then to dress their pictures. Talk about the colour of their skin, their hairstyle and their features. They can be asked questions like:

- What is the same about you and the rest of the class?

- What is different about you that makes you who you are – makes you special?

- When done, mount and display at an accessible height so children can re-visit their work.

Making books

Each child contributes a page or two to the book the group is making, or makes their own: as they prefer. Ask children to bring in photographs of themselves and their families and pictures from magazines which they can use as well as their own drawings to illustrate the book. Those who can write in a language other than English should be encouraged to do so. The books could include the food they like to eat, the games they like to play, and the things that make them happy, sad or angry.

Making books about family members provides opportunities to talk about who they are and what they do inside and outside the home. This can be useful for highlighting sex roles and similarities and differences between families.

Making books about their favourite Persona Doll can deepen children's bonding with the Doll.

Involve the children in setting up a display of their books. Showing it to children and teachers from other classes can help boost children's confidence and self-esteem. Parents too could be invited to see what their children have created.

Communicating without words

Brainstorm the different ways in which, without speaking, we show other people what we want, how we are feeling and what we are going to do. Encourage the children to act out feelings using their faces and bodies. Invite someone in to talk to the children about Braille and to show them examples. Somebody else could come and tell them about Sign language and teach them a few signs.

Invite parents who speak languages other than English to teach the children a few phrases or short songs. Children who speak two or more languages could be asked if they would like to teach everyone how to say a few words, like goodbye, hello, good morning, good night in their home language(s).

Display books in a range of languages, including Sign, Braille and dual text books.

Handling conflict

Children sit in a circle and talk about times when they have found it hard to share. Choose a few of their experiences to be role-played – ask permission from the affected children first. To bring children out of role, clap at the end and thank the children by name. Then ask them how they felt when they were acting and whether their problem could have been resolved in a different way. The rest of the group can be encouraged to talk about what they think each person felt and how they felt when watching the role-play and possible alternative solutions can be discussed.

These two tasks are drawn from Claire and Holden (2007:36)

> **Donkeys**: This can only really be done once with each group of children. Two volunteers come up to act as donkeys (they might wear donkey ears). They are lightly tied together to stop the donkeys straying) and shown two bowls of fruit on opposite sides of the room. Invariably, a tug of war develops. Before the stronger child can reach the fruit, stop the struggle and ask the group

what can be done to solve their problem. Collect suggestions until a child comes up with a co-operative solution: then let the donkeys carry it out and share the fruit around the class.

Solutions: Each group of four to six children is given a card with a familiar conflict situation written on it. Some examples:

■ on TV: A wants to watch a cartoon but B wants to watch a game show which is on at the same time

■ at the fair: A wants to go on the roller coaster but B doesn't and A doesn't want to go on it alone

■ both A and B want the same reading book

The children brainstorm as many solutions as possible and a member of the group writes down the suggestions. The class then comes together to look at all the different solutions to the various problems and decides which they think would work best.

Critiquing stories

You'll need books in which issues are appropriately and sensitively explored and which have strong central characters. A creative way to develop critical awareness could be to dramatise stories and encourage the children to act out alternative story lines or endings. Ask questions to help the children empathise with the characters that have been treated unfairly, reflect on what they've read or have had read to them, think about the way the characters acted and consider alternative endings.

■ Is there a character in the story you would like to be your friend? Why?

■ Is there a character in the story you would not want to be friends with? Why?

■ Is there any character in the story that you think was treated unfairly?

■ What do you think about the way the story ends?

■ Can you suggest a different ending?

■ What do you like (not like) about the illustrations?

■ How did the story and the illustrations make you feel?

Remembering

Children spend a few moments remembering a time when they were unfairly treated. How it made them feel and what, if anything, was done about it.

They then share their memory with their neighbour and how they felt.

Sharing experiences during feedback can deepen understanding and strengthen determination to challenge unfairness in settings/schools and outside them.

Talking about their feelings can reinforce the messages of the Persona Doll stories – if certain words or actions upset them, they might also upset other children.

The task could be ended with this old Chinese proverb:

> People will forget what you said ...
> People will forget what you did ...
> But people will never forget how you made them feel.

Persona Doll stories – some questions for educators to think about

During Persona Doll storytelling sessions do we run the risk of suggesting that unsolvable personal and social problems can be fixed by talking about them?

To create stories that reflect children's experiences, we need to observe children closely and listen more carefully to their conversations. Are we trespassing on their privacy?

How can we engage children during Persona Doll storytelling sessions when they are at the early stages of learning English as an additional language? From their point of view very little happens. The Doll just sits on the educator's lap doing nothing, the educator and the children talk, but most of it is meaningless and there are few visual clues.

How would you have responded if you were telling a Persona Doll story and a child said something that left you flabbergasted? These comments were made by children during Persona Doll story-sessions:

> We can't be friends with children in wheelchairs because they can't play.

You know something funny? My friend hasn't got a dad at her house: she's got two mums.

My gran says I mustn't play with Black children: they smell.

My mum's gone away and she's never coming back.

My grandpa's in heaven. But Joel at my school said there isn't a place called heaven.

My dad hit my mum again last night.

5

A dream comes true

Since the setting up of Persona Doll Training in Britain in March 2000, Carol Smith and I have had a dream. The dream became a reality when Carol returned to Cape Town in September 2003 and Persona Doll Training South Africa was born.

Eager to put into practice everything she had learned from delivering Persona Doll training in Britain, Australia, New Zealand, Iceland and Berlin, Carol was also keen to ensure that the project would have a distinctive South African character.

In her words:

> The Persona Doll approach builds on the African belief in *Ubuntu* (*motho ke motho ka batho ba bang* – a person is a person through other people) and the universal and African traditions of storytelling, building this empathy, and then taking it a step further into problem solving discussion. The focus is on the importance of hearing children's and adults' voices, respecting diversity and 'unlearning' discrimination. The Dolls are a practical tool with which to implement Nelson Mandela's belief that: No one is born hating another person because of the colour of their skin, or their background, or their religion. People must learn to hate, and if they can learn to hate, they can be taught to love.

The objectives are to:

- train, empower and support practitioners, lecturers and trainers to implement the Persona Doll approach

■ set up a doll-making project to produce Persona Dolls and to skill women from deprived communities that have high levels of un-employment

■ adapt and develop Persona Doll Training materials for South Africa

■ research and evaluate the project

The approach is fully consistent with the revised schools' curriculum which states that: 'Prejudice, often in the form of racism, is still present in post-apartheid South Africa. These prejudices must be acknow-ledged and challenged if they are to be overcome.'

Conditions in the UK are radically different from those in South Africa, a country emerging from decades of apartheid and oppression. Women and children are the most vulnerable groups. The South African Con-stitution and the Bill of Rights (1996) outlaws discrimination on the basis of race, culture, faith, gender, sexual orientation and disability. The problem is that because of the general ignorance and prejudice, many teachers and trainers are ill-equipped to deal with equality, in-clusion and diversity issues. They are seeking answers: 'Our children won't go near others with HIV/AIDS, I don't know what to do.' 'Racism is rife in our school.' 'Sexism is a huge problem'. They welcome the sup-port and guidance Persona Doll training provides and appreciate that the Dolls are not toys but props to engage children in active learning through story and dialogue. As one teacher affirms: 'This is a com-pletely non-threatening way to talk about equality issues – the Dolls make it easy to open up. The approach is creative, stimulating and fun.'

One of Carol's first tasks was to set up a Doll making facility. Unlike in the UK, much of the buying of the Dolls has to be heavily subsidised because most settings, schools and community organisations do not have the money to pay for them.

Doll making

Juanita Bosch manages and oversees the manufacture of the Dolls. She has always shown a keen interest in crafts as well as in the social development of adults and children: 'My reason for getting involved in the Doll making business was a fascination for cloth dolls since I was small. I always wanted to make cloth Dolls and when Carol approached me in 2004 about this project, I responded immediately.'

'Culture has changed people – they have to change'

'Another thing I have learnt about is gender, issues of gender, homosexual: and heterosexual I didn't know anything about this'

'It was amazing how everyone worked with the Dolls, even the men!'

Commenting on the Dolls, teachers said:

We are very stressed at school but we fought to come to this workshop. The Dolls de-stress and energise us

The Dolls helped me to identify with other people's experiences

Some shy children have started to speak up and they keep asking when the Doll will visit again

Also Dolls help me to plan and give the true information and relate to young people more and more

The Persona Dolls can be used to dig the hidden information from the child. These Dolls also help to pull out the strengths that a child has

Before I used to think Dolls were useless things but now I know and I feel that they are carrying power to influence

The children listen in a different way now – they are so involved and curious

Case Study
A teacher with more than twelve years teaching experience reports that Molly, her Persona Doll, frequently visits her class of boisterous four year olds and has enabled her to tackle tricky social issues:

Molly looks so lifelike that the children treat her like a friend. She has her own identity and we've created a whole story around her. She lives in nearby Sun Valley with her family and faces challenges similar to those our children deal with so through her we are able to address their issues. I bring Molly into the group, sit her on my knee, tell the children she's having a problem with bullying, for instance and I ask them what advice they have for her. This is usually the start of a lively discussion with the children giving suggestions or sharing their stories. Somehow, if Molly says that she hates being bullied and feels frightened, it's easier for the other kids to open up. It also empowers them when they come up with solutions that they can imagine being implemented. And when it's time to go, all the kids want to give her a big hug.

Juanita has trained three groups of unskilled women and a few men. All are from deprived communities with high unemployment and many are HIV positive. Their work provides much needed income for their families as they are the sole bread winners. They produce all the Dolls for the project – on average about 500 per year. They also make the dresses, knickers, jeans, trousers, school uniforms, headscarves and T-shirts for the Dolls. And that's not all. A large number of the UK Persona Dolls are dressed in clothes these South African Doll-making groups have made.

Carol has run workshops for the groups so they know how the Dolls they make are being used. Through the group they have been em-powered and learned new skills: their newly found confidence is tangible.

The training
Organisations, schools, universities and colleges are charged for train-ing according to their individual circumstances: some are able to pay the full fee while others pay very little or nothing at all. In the beginning most of the training took place in Cape Town and the surrounding areas but since then it has spread to other parts of this vast country. To ensure that it is delivered in the dominant language of a particular area, Carol's team consists of part-time trainers who are able to speak a range of lan-guages. There are 11 official languages in South Africa: some are more widely spoken than others and many people speak and understand more than one.

The training helps to raise awareness of human rights issues, builds confidence and gives participants the skills they need to confront the bigotry and the internalised oppression that all South Africans carry. In schools in urban and rural areas which are characterised by deprivation and great poverty as well as in those in wealthy, well-resourced, high status middle class neighbourhoods, bullying, exclusion, fighting and teasing linked to racism, sexism, xenophobia and HIV/AIDS are commonplace. It also raises teachers' awareness of the importance of talking about their own and the children's feelings and learning how to use Persona Dolls to address difficult issues like HIV and AIDS in a non-threatening and constructive way.

Support visits help to ensure that what is learnt at the training is implemented and to motivate people to start working with the Dolls. The visits are particularly valuable when they involve teachers who have varying levels of training, experience and skills.

Pre-school teachers in community based centres, primary school teachers, social workers, psychologists, childcare workers and toy library workers are all being trained by Persona Doll trainers. In order to reach as many children as possible Carol and her team also run training the trainer courses for non-governmental organisations, colleges and universities who then integrate the Persona Doll approach into their ongoing accredited in-service training programmes. A training of trainers resource pack has been developed in English and translated into Afrikaans and Xhosa, the dominant languages in the Cape, for all trainers to use.

An important breakthrough occurred in 2004/5. The Western Cape Education Department and Persona Doll Training launched the Valley Life Skills Pilot Project to train teachers working with children from aged 3 to 9 and Family and Community Motivators on how to use Persona Dolls, particularly in relation to the stigma attached to HIV/AIDS. Research confirms the need to address discrimination against children and adults with HIV/AIDS because children are denied access to schooling and those who are admitted frequently face exclusion by other pupils.

The power of the Dolls is captured in this email sent by Carol:

> Absolutely fantastic feedback from schools at a follow up workshop yesterday. At one school in Gugulethu the parents said NO we don't want our kids to know about AIDS! The school organised a meeting – got huge attendance and did a Persona Doll session with the parents being 'children'. It was fantastic! The teachers were SO excited because the parents said YES if that's how you do it please DO it. Luckily a person from the Education Department was there to see it all!

Training has been extended to include more teachers and childcare workers and workshops held to support those who had previously been trained. In recognition of this work Persona Doll Training was selected to make a partnership submission with the Western Cape Education Department for the Commonwealth Countries Good Practice Awards

(2007). The partnership was also shortlisted for the Western Premiers Service Excellence Awards in 2008. They didn't win but among the finalists.

Teachers reported that when they used the Dolls to implement the skills learning programme, the atmosphere was happier and livelier, children showed greater interest and participated more actively, concentrated better, were more curious than usual and there was a in problem solving, confidence and language development. Some teachers found that there was less aggression and a calmer atmosphere when the Dolls visited. Teachers are becoming more aware of the fact that the way they behave and model respectful interaction with children has a powerful effect. The Dolls are helping teacher-child and child-child relationships with regard to respect and care.

In settings and schools in the UK it is generally agreed that the educator's job is to support children by asking questions, listening and talking to them, rather than simply feeding them knowledge and skills. In South Africa one debilitating effect of the anti-education apartheid inheritance is a workforce of de-motivated, under-qualified, unconfident, dependent teachers. And yet in the course of their training and support work, Carol and her team have met exceptional teachers who teach classes of 40-90 children with few resources and do it with no support or assistance. They also care for the children and give of their own time and money to promote their all round development. But they are the exception not the rule. For the majority, attending Persona Doll training sessions and being supported to work with the Dolls has been stimulating, and for some, a far-reaching and profound experience.

Some personal responses from teachers to the training and the Dolls:

> A woman in Cape Town came to Carol in a shaky state, after a session, to say 'I have never spoken to anyone about that childhood incident before'

> An older mixed race woman in Cape Town wept, telling about forced removals in her childhood, and her fear of Black people

> A male participant said: 'If you cry there is something that is a relief to yourself and you feel free. And children love to talk about their feelings so that they can feel relief'

A typical persona

Nobuhle is the name of this girl and she is 4 years old. She speaks isiXhosa and her clan name is Mambhele. She lives with her grandmother, uncle and cousins in a two-roomed shack. Her mother is a domestic worker far away from home. She shares a bed with her grandmother and another cousin. Every night before they sleep her grandmother tells them a traditional story.

Nobuhle attends pre-school in Khayelitsha near where she lives. After school or during week-ends she helps her grandmother wash dishes and the clothes. She likes to play hide and seek with her cousins and friends and to share her favourite meal *umgqusho* with them. When they get tired of playing, they watch TV programmes especially *Takalani Sesame*. She doesn't like violence and fighting [she hears fighting noises at night] and she fears fire.

In a secondary school

Not only primary school teachers are working with the Dolls. A secondary school life orientation teacher used them very effectively with a group of 14 year olds. He changed the approach slightly. Small groups of six teenagers created the Dolls' personas and solved problems based on their life situations. They responded with empathy, spoke freely about the issues as they were not on the spot personally and came up with realistic ideas for solving problems and providing support. Through the Dolls, the teacher was able to address issues of privacy, addiction and sexual awareness. One of the teenagers said, 'I am late for school every day because I must wait in line for the one communal toilet that has a lock – I can't get dressed at home in our shack because my mother's boyfriend is always there'.

This work was written up as a case study for a training manual for secondary educators.

Persona Dolls in the community

There is a great need for psychosocial care and learning for young children and adults. Persona Dolls have proved to be a practical and effective tool to use in communities where unemployment, poverty, crime and violence are commonplace. The group Family and Community Motivators work at a local level with families, the most vulnerable children and their primary caregivers. Most young children in South Africa do not have access to organised early childhood development pro-grammes and many who enter the school system do not make ade-quate progress: their high drop-out rate by Grade 2 (7-8 year olds) is of grave concern.

The training Carol and her team are providing for Family and Com-munity Motivators addresses difficult issues around HIV and AIDS in a non-threatening and constructive way. Some participants had avoided talking about the subject before the training and one described how the Persona Doll is helping her: 'When I am feeling anxious, I make eye con-tact with the Doll then I can speak about AIDS and carry on.'

Family and Community Motivators are now using Persona Dolls as part of their work.

The team are also training childcare workers, volunteers and com-munity workers in rural areas in other parts of South Africa who provide home-based care, support for orphans and vulnerable children. These children have lost parents, or may lose them in the near or medium future. The childcare workers make daily home visits to designated orphaned homes to develop the fortitude of the orphans, visit them in the morning before school, ensure they go to school, help with home-work, check they have clothes, guide them and develop their life skills.

Some concerns emerged in the training of childcare workers, such as:

■ uneasiness about cultures in transition and coping with new in-fluences

■ challenging gender issues in the context of traditional African culture and traditionally taught roles. Conflict arises for example around the traditional condemnation of homosexuality and the South African Constitution which outlaws discrimination on the grounds of sexual orientation

■ the link between HIV and poverty, ie young women and girls being seduced into having sex in return for food and believing they'll be cared for. This often results in their contracting HIV/AIDS

■ gender education and the implications for HIV/AIDS including what boys are apparently being taught at initiation schools such as the still prevalent myth that having sex with a virgin cures AIDS

These are some of the issues that the Dolls are helping to address. Many reflect the huge social problems that decades of oppression, brutalisation and poverty have generated:

- HIV/AIDS, stigma and awareness of the issues
- racism and xenophobia
- albinism
- poverty
- violence issues: gangs, street violence, rape
- gender issues: stereotyping, discrimination and sexuality
- sexual abuse of children
- physical abuse of children
- teenage pregnancy
- disability
- discrimination: culture, language and race
- not understanding children's rights
- drugs and alcohol
- orphans and households headed by children
- divorce, single parents, absent fathers
- abandonment
- fear
- hygiene: lack of information
- lack of emotional support
- bereavement
- lack of self awareness

It is a depressing list. But the Persona Doll approach is becoming widely understood and implemented in South Africa. Persona Doll Training is one of the few organisations where the focus is clearly on promoting anti-discrimination and helping adults and children to unlearn the prejudices and bigotry they have been exposed to for so many years. The Dolls are really helping to make a difference in South Africa and they certainly keep Carol and me hopeful and positive about the future.

6

The Dolls are special and
so are the trainers

I have argued throughout this book that Persona Dolls can promote equality and social justice while countering prejudice and discrimination and that they need to be used by people who are skilled, knowledgeable, respectful and empathetic. This requires dedication and commitment – as Castro said: 'The road is long and patience is needed'. But as the brief personal accounts which follow show, the journey is also a learning, rewarding and stimulating experience.

Sue

Working for Persona Dolls has made me reflect on a number of discriminatory issues that had not occurred to me before. One of the most challenging aspects has been the privilege of sharing the personal stories of practitioners on the course: some of these have been heart-rending, others have shown how deeply the knife goes in when a person's self-esteem is destroyed, often through a seemingly trivial act of name calling, and how the wound can be carried into adulthood, and sometimes surprises the victim who thinks that past experiences have no more power to hurt.

One of the most heartening aspects is hearing how people have recognised their own stereotyping through a particular incident and have been amazed at how narrow-minded they had been before. Two incidents were recalled in training sessions concerning Travellers. One teacher was nervous about visiting a Traveller site and asked someone from the Traveller education service to accompany her. She was astounded on entering the child's trailer to see that it was immaculate. She was given tea and made to feel very welcome: she confessed her shame as she realised what her expectations had been.

The other was from a nursery teacher who discovered one morning that some trailers had been parked on the public car park in front of the nursery and the parents were finding it difficult to park to deliver and pick up their children. Somewhat fearfully the teacher approached the Traveller families and asked if they would park their trailers to one side so that others could have access. This was done with no fuss, and when a few days later, over a weekend, the Travellers moved on, the teacher arrived especially early on the Monday morning, as she anticipated a mess to clear up. Again, she was chastened to find the site beautifully clean and all the rubbish neatly bagged up.

C. S. Lewis said 'if you think you are not conceited, it means you are very conceited indeed'. I think the same is true of prejudice. I try to encourage people on training to face up to their prejudices, because we all have them. The important thing is to be honest with ourselves and to begin to deal with the issues that so destroy our own lives and the lives of those around us. Persona Dolls have proved time and again to be an effective tool for helping young children especially, to recognise how their words and actions can hurt other people. As they talk about how others might feel, they can begin to express their own emotions and consider how things can be put right. Adults challenged by their victims later in life are often horrified by the pain they caused and of which they were unaware at the time ... 'but we were only children, we were just playing.' I hope that Persona Dolls can help the next generation of children to put themselves in another's shoes, to support the vulnerable and to grow up to understand that, although we are not all the same, we are all equal, and that diversity is something to be truly celebrated.

I feel privileged to have worked with the Dolls and I continue to learn with the children, the practitioners and my colleagues. I have made some discoveries about myself which are uncomfortable, but it's a journey I know I must continue to make.

Ruth

How did my journey begin? 1977 and the punk explosion onto the music scene and the Rock against Racism march and concert in London, travelling by coach from Bradford for the day, outrageously dressed and ready for an exciting day. I remember the march was massive and slowed down as we marched through National Front strongholds with them shouting abuse at us.

1980 – finally qualified as a teacher and got my first job in a Language Centre in Bradford teaching English as a second language. Teachers from primary schools came to visit to see how children acquired language using the very boring, Keystone Approach. One of them was horrified that the children were not speaking English to each other and the headteacher saying, 'How on earth do you expect them to communicate?' Comments being made when we took the children into town on a public bus, 'I'm not sending my child to that Paki school.'

1986 – attending my first Women and Girls in Education conference in Bradford and being amongst like-minded women and having my awareness raised about gender issues. After that conference I facilitated a workshop at a weekend course on Girl Only Groups.

1987 – a group of teachers decided to meet once a week to discuss 'race' and gender issues and to try and develop our own resources. Seven of us were then seconded for one day a week for a year to produce a practical guide to combat discrimination in the classroom and across all aspects of the curriculum. We produced this book but then the Conservatives took over Bradford Council, all funding for publication was withdrawn and we became disillusioned.

I continued my own personal awareness raising with colleagues and children, for instance ensuring that the school library had a wide range of books depicting girls and Black children in positive roles and getting rid of overtly racist and sexist books. I also ran whole school assemblies to show women in non-traditional roles. My nursery nurse rode a motorbike to school so for one assembly, dressed in her leathers, she brought her bike into the hall and asked the children questions about parts of the bike and safety measures. I was also lucky that one of the children in my class had a mother who was a wrestler. So I asked her to come in and show the children some moves and how to fall safely. Imagine my delight when she turned up with her friend, Klondyke Kate and they performed a mini-wrestling match. You could have heard a pin drop: that was the quietest assembly of children ever!

2001 and I was inspired by the Persona Doll Training run by Carol and Babette in Bradford and applied to become a trainer. I wanted to continue challenging discrimination and diversity and saw this as a way of raising awareness with early years practitioners and a brilliant idea to get young children to begin to discuss these issues. When I got the job one of my best friends said, 'I'm so proud of you Ruth. You're continuing what we stared all those years ago.' I learnt a lot from Carol with whom I delivered training – she dealt with comments from participants succinctly and in a way that made people look at things differently.

Here are a few anecdotes from training sessions.

- a room full of women none of whom could think of a time in their lives when they had been discriminated against. I asked if they had ever been to a car showroom, a shop or pub with a male friend, where the assumption was made that he was buying the car, paying for the goods, getting the drinks

- a girl in Bradford said that she had once worked at Tesco. A family refused to have her serve them because she was a 'Paki'. Tesco's response was to let a White member of staff serve them instead!

- A stereotype that often comes up when creating personas for Chinese Dolls is that they live in Chinese restaurants or takeaways. Others around disability, gender and same sex parents are rife.

By talking about the Dolls we have in our children centre, their personas, why we chose them and how we use them, I hope participants reflect on and change their stereotypical thinking. I hope I am continuing to challenge discrimination in my life – socially and professionally.

Meryl

For participants having the opportunity to reflect on their own practice is valuable particularly as it is often ignored in the work place due to time constraints. Reflecting on personal values and stereotypes is even less considered. Persona Doll training offers the opportunity to do both of these important things in a safe, supportive environment, often for the first time. As I travel around the country delivering training I am struck by the patterns that emerge in rooms full of mostly female early years' practitioners, overwhelmingly white (outside London), always interested, engaged and willing to be challenged.

Training days in particular, but workshops too, can be challenging experiences for participants particularly if they have never before considered issues such as the ones we explore. This is what happens regularly and I personally love it. Participants challenge my thinking and I theirs.

Only this week smoking arose as an issue. A participant relayed to the rest of us how excluded she is made to feel, even though she agrees with the smoking ban and willingly takes herself outside to smoke. Other smokers described what it felt like to be picked on, to be made to feel dirty and outside the majority. As a group we then considered that if smokers felt this excluded, how might ethnic minorities feel? Challenging stuff!

At Persona Doll training sessions I have been asked, 'but what's wrong with calling it the Paki shop, everyone calls it that?' Unpicking the nuances of such ingrained terminology is sensitive and challenging and needs to be discussed because how exactly do you comment on, red, auburn, titian, or ginger hair, and which description is correct? Similarly, how do we describe our plump, chunky, oversized, fat or cuddly Persona Dolls? We do not all agree on the terms, some of us are offended, some of us are uncomfortable so do not use such terms and the question of political correctness always arises. In this spirit of supportive reflective discussion we begin to consider how others might feel and why or how we hold the views that we do.

I have learnt so much about myself and early years practice as a Persona Doll trainer. My own personal interest springs from a lifetime of being particularly visible as I am a Grenadian, black, British, female, early years practitioner. I have often been the only non-white practitioner in the early years settings I have worked in. In over thirty years of working I have seen both good and bad scenarios and use many of them as illustrations when training. My particular area of interest is ethnicity and raising awareness of good anti-discriminatory practice amongst students and practitioners which compliments my work as a Persona Doll trainer.

Meredith

Can't remember when I didn't adopt an anti-discriminatory way of working as I've always worked in multicultural schools and have had a leaning towards and responsibility for the PSHCE side of the curriculum. Had some training in the 1980s, but also remember feeling it was rather patronising as I thought the information was already well known and in practice.

Over the years in my various jobs colleagues have largely supported my anti-discriminatory perspective. I have had to work hard to instil pro-active rather than re-active approaches and we can become a little complacent at times. My own commitment has kept me going, which is a lot to do with having a special needs child myself I think and always being a person who relates to the struggler rather than to the winner. I started using Persona Dolls after attending a day's training in Leicester run by Carol and Babette.

Being a Persona Doll trainer has been a thoroughly positive experience, getting to know the other trainers and feeling that almost all participants leave the day's training with a smile. It has made me firm up my thinking on anti-discriminatory issues, reflect more deeply and be more able to express myself confidently about possibly sensitive areas.

Meeta

I came to Britain as a refugee in 1971 when Idi Amin expelled thousands of Asians from Uganda, East Africa. Asian immigrants immediately became targets of racist abuse and sometimes assault. I was 8 years old when I started at the local primary school. Other children spoke to me as if I was stupid simply because I was a different colour from them. In fact, I spoke perfect English as I was educated in English in Uganda. When I was out with my family, we were often called names and told to go 'back home'. I didn't quite know where home actually was. As far as I know there was no anti-discriminatory teaching in schools. How wonderful it would have been to have Persona Dolls in schools in those days. Children were growing up with negative stereotypes which were reinforced by a culture that thought that the *Black and White Minstrels* were entertainment and that *Love Thy Neighbour* was comedy.

I discovered Persona Dolls as a tool for anti-discriminatory teaching whilst teaching at a multicultural Early Years Centre in Slough in 2001. I attended a training session run by Babette and remember being blown away by what I experienced. Since then I have used Persona Dolls with small children to address a range of issues such as name calling, cultural stereotyping and understanding the experiences and needs of refugees. The Dolls became friends of the group and shared happy and sad times with us. I am still amazed at how children understand the plight of others through the Dolls and genuinely offer suggestions to help them. I feel the Dolls helped the children recognise unfairness and learn the skills they need to challenge it.

I am now the Training Administrator for Persona Doll training and receive enquiries and requests for training from local authorities, colleges/universities and a range of early years settings and schools. More recently, individual practitioners who do not have access to training in their area have contacted me and I have put them in touch with local authorities where in-house training was on offer.

To my delight I have recently received enquiries from enthusiastic colleagues in America and Iceland. A request for Persona Doll training for all the staff of a Kindergarten in Iceland resulted in their booking a hotel conference room in London and having the training delivered to them there.

A teacher from Iceland told me:

> I think the reason you are getting more and more interest from Iceland is that the groups you have already had have such a good experience from your training. This is a small community and good news travels.

Also Iceland has had a huge increase in immigration and there is an awakening on working with children to encourage tolerance for different people, ideas and cultures.

I think my job as training administrator plays a part, however small, in the continuing struggle for equality and a world free from discrimination. It is good working with progressive people to effect positive change.

Marie

I began working in the Ethnic Minority Achievement Service in 1998 and so you could say that that was when I began working in an anti-discriminatory way. I chose to work with the Portsmouth Team after finding that EAL pupils needs were not being met effectively in secondary schools and I felt that I could make a difference by working with children from ethnic minority backgrounds. It was very gratifying to see children grow in confidence and understanding when they received appropriate support.

I have been working in the primary sector only since moving to Swindon in 2003 and have found children's responses to the Dolls quite illuminating. They can engage at a very mature level with the situations in which the Dolls find themselves and have proved to be very capable of empathy and a desire to help the Doll to solve her/his specific problem. Using the Dolls in conjunction with the SEAL (Social and Emotional Aspects of Learning) materials has been particularly successful in both primary and Year 7 secondary phase for anti-bullying work, racist or otherwise. From an inclusion point of view the resource is considered invaluable to practitioners and teachers of Early Years Foundation Stage pupils.

Being a Persona Doll Trainer has been especially significant for me because it has highlighted the importance of educating children at a very early age to challenge injustice. Training is always well received by all practitioners who can immediately see the application of the method to their settings: they express this with great enthusiasm.

Jane

I should have grown up being the most racist person going! It's funny how life experience changes attitudes and opinions. You see my mother and father both lived in Birmingham in the aftermath of the First World War and then struggled through the Second World War. My sister had to go to boarding school so that my mother could do her bit in a factory making spitfires. The result was that they hated anyone from the enemy countries with a vengeance and even Americans who came to 'claim victory at the last minute when all the fighting was over'. People from the Caribbean then came to live in areas of Birmingham, followed by the Asian community. These were all people to be avoided: they smelt of garlic and chillies and were dirty. Don't get me wrong. I loved my Mum and Dad to bits but their experience of life was marred by the death of loved ones, poverty and misjudgements. They were as kind as anyone could be to family and friends and would have given me their life if need be. I grew up with all these prejudices not only from my parents but from my relations too.

I must admit I was puzzled by these judgements and when I went to university I lived in a diverse student community and began to think that the judgements you make about people should be based on their character and the way they live their lives not on their nationality or culture. Then when I came to live in Yorkshire and to teach in inner city schools and children's centres I really found an understanding of different cultures and socio-economic circumstances. I had a clearer picture of life and how many judgements are made without understanding. I now try to portray a clear picture of the need to reflect and live diversity throughout your practice in the settings I visit and in the courses I run and try to give young children clear values to live by. Persona Dolls have helped me on my journey and, as a trainer I hope I can help others.

Carol

Growing up as a privileged white South African in Cape Town during apartheid I always felt I was missing out on something – Africa perhaps? My early contact with people who were different from myself were Black and Mixed Race domestic workers. I often sought their company and felt uncomfortable about their roles. I remember always being angry about unfairness and injustice and this gave me the confidence to challenge. In the 60s and 70s in South Africa there was a lot to be angry about: pass laws, the immorality act, whites only beaches and the rest. In this I was encouraged by my parents who were always fair and by my school experiences. Going to an anti-government white church school led to exposure to black schools and sport visits to black townships: experiences never allowed under apartheid at white state schools.

My personal experiences of bullying by teachers and children reinforced my feelings of empathy for the outsider and the underdog.

My first teaching job was as a teacher in a non-racial preschool with diverse cultures and languages in Namibia in the late 1970s, a great learning experience. I then welcomed an opportunity to help start and teach on an early years teacher training course in one of the apartheid homelands which miraculously had at that time a progressive Education Department. I learnt such a lot from the Tswana tribal authorities and from the rural women who ran the crèches, some with no water, little food, a couple of toys and loads of enthusiasm. My next move was into Early Childhood Development (ECD) work in Cape Town. Development and human rights always appealed more than the curriculum work. I became involved in anti-apartheid women's and children's rights organisations.

Then through an old friend and colleague, Helen Robb, I was introduced to the concept of anti-bias. Suddenly it all made sense. ECD and activism came together: teachers can be change agents and challenge racism, sexism and other social oppressions actively. I was inspired by Louise Derman-Sparks who spoke at an ECD anti-bias conference in Cape Town in the mid 1990s. I connected with Babette in London and through her discovered in March 2000 the fantastic Persona Dolls. I was excited by the power of the Dolls, their non-threatening aspect that they gave equalities work a real focus. Training with first Babette, and then with Sue and Ruth in the UK was a great learning experience and fun.

I returned to Cape Town in 2003 to establish Persona Doll Training South Africa. I am at present undertaking a research project examining Persona Dolls and anti-bias curriculum practice with young children: A South African case study.

Eight years later I am still excited about the powerful Persona Dolls.

Babette

I was on the antiracist road from an early age partly because of my parents' encouragement but also because I glimpsed how Black South Africans were being treated and heard the racist language of my extended family, other adults and my peers. 1963, involvement in the liberation struggle forced my husband and me to come to London with our four children. Active links with home were provided by our membership of the local branch of the ANC, the African National Congress and the Anti-Apartheid movement.

It was only in the mid-1970s when teaching on an Nursery Nursing course (then very racist, sexist, and classist) that I became actively involved in confronting racism in this country. An invitation by Jane Lane, a leading authority on racial equality in the early years, to join a group of like-minded people proved over the next few years to be a most amazing learning, consciousness-raising, motivating and sometimes painful experience .

On taking early retirement, I became the Co-ordinator of the Early Years Trainers Anti-Racist Network, (EYTARN) and one of its trainers which was another learning experience. As the EYTARN representative on a European Early Years Network, I discovered Persona Dolls!

Setting up the charity and doing the training has been the most rewarding experience crowned only by Carol establishing Persona Doll Training in South Africa.

In all the years that I have been involved in promoting equity and inclusion while challenging discrimination, particularly racism, I have not come across a tool as powerful as the Dolls. Participants, through bonding and identifying with them, seem to be more receptive and willing to engage than during traditional anti-discriminatory training. In their small way Persona Dolls and their stories are contributing to the creation of a society in which Martin Luther King's famous dream could be attainable:

> I have a dream that my four little children will one day live in a nation where they will not be judged by the colour of their skin but by their character. ... I have a dream that one day ... little black boys and black girls will be able to join hands with little white boys and white girls as sisters and brothers.

7

Persona Dolls under
the microscope

One of the joys of writing this book has been re-visiting Professor
Glenda MacNaughton's ground-breaking Persona Doll research
project (1999) and discovering a school-based study undertaken by Elaine McClement and an action research project conducted
by Eve Cook. The later pieces of research were completed in 2004 and
mirror some of MacNaughton's findings.

These studies have backed up my belief that the Dolls are powerful, that
in their child-friendly way they encourage children to express their
thoughts, attitudes and feelings. It is so confirming and reassuring to
know that what was previously anecdote and speculation is now supported by research on the ground. I feel sure that as more and more
university and college lecturers introduce Persona Dolls to their students, a good many will opt to base their research projects around
them. I suspect that students from a range of disciplines will be attrac-
ted by the potential the Dolls offer. It may be that the research by
McClement and Cook represents the tip of an iceberg, and that there is
a body of work out there that we know nothing about.

Taking a closer look

The Australian Equity and Social Diversity Research project led by
MacNaughton used Persona Dolls to try and uncover young children's
prejudices and discriminatory attitudes and to promote a sense of fairness and justice. It gives adults an opportunity to hear directly from the

children what they think and feel about themselves and other people. This is important because in too many research projects, as Cannella (1998:10) said: 'the most critical voices that are silent in our constructions of early childhood education are the children with whom we work. Our constructions of research have not fostered methods that facilitate hearing their voices'.

The aims of the project were to:

■ find out what 4 and 5 year-old children knew about race, class and gender when she and her co-researcher first met them

■ use the Dolls and their stories to positively introduce a range of equity and social diversity issues to the children

■ evaluate if and how the Dolls and their stories changed what the children knew

The children were interviewed and asked semi-structured questions. The four Dolls acted as ice-breakers, helping to keep the children's conversations focused and providing opportunities for the researchers to tell stories around class, 'race' and gender issues. The children were encouraged to play with the four Dolls:

> Shiree, a girl from an Aboriginal-Australian family.
> Willie, a boy from a Vietnamese-Australian family.
> Olivia, a girl from a rich Anglo-Australian family.
> Tom, a boy from a poor Anglo-Australian family.

The focus of the research was on comparing and exploring the differences and similarities between the silences and voices of 4 and 5 year-old Anglo-Australian and Vietnamese-Australian children. The approach was based on the work of Jonathon Silin (1999:44) who suggests that: 'Silence can signal resistance as well as oppression, voice can create new moments for social control as well as for personal efficacy. And words are notorious for concealing and transforming as well as revealing the truth of our lives'. The co-researcher in the project, Heather, was able to wait patiently for children to answer her questions. Instead of jumping to the conclusion that their failure to respond always signified indifference, shyness or ignorance, she read the silence which often greeted her questions to mean that they were thinking hard about what she had asked them. The following exchange captures how valuing silences can elicit important information about how young children think about the complex issues of diversity:

Heather: I'm just wondering what you know about Aboriginal people. 'Cause you noticed when you came in that this was a different doll, didn't you? You noticed that ... [long pause waiting for child]

Jane: And, sometimes they make houses and sometimes they move on, because um they make it out of sticks and leaves. And also Aboriginals will

[very long pause]

Heather: Anything else you can think of about Aboriginals that you know about?

Jane: Nope. And sometimes Aboriginals also um they also um Aboriginals [pause]

Researcher: What about you? Do you know anybody Aboriginal? Do you know any Aboriginal people?

Jane: Two.

Heather: You know two. Oh I see.

Jane: Boory and ah Bill Hiney.

Heather: And where do they live?

Jane: Um they live in Melbourne.

Heather: They live in Melbourne.

[Long pause waiting for child to continue]

Jane: But I also know that um a long, long time ago that the white people um took their children, the Aboriginal children away from their mum and dad because they thought that they weren't treating them well. And also I think [pause Heather waits]

Heather: Anything else? You're trying so hard to remember. We'll talk about something else and if you happen to remember anything that you wanted to say you can just tell me. Okay.

Heather's patience encouraged Jane to reveal that she knew more about Aboriginal people than she at first let on. The researchers would not have known that she knew anything about the 'stolen generations' – the practice of forcefully removing Aboriginal children from their families and placing them in White Australian homes. MacNaughton believes that although Jane's knowledge is uncertain, she is working hard to construct meanings about Aboriginal people and their lives in the past and in the here and now. The meanings she is giving to the word Aboriginal also shows that young children can develop understandings of complex contemporary issues and show empathy for the pain of others. There is much that can be added to her learning but at the age of 4 she has already understood that there is more to being Aboriginal than skin colour.

However, most of the Anglo-Australian children's understandings about Aboriginal Australians were *mis*understandings and many children knew little or nothing about these indigenous peoples and their culture. Common to the children who did have some knowledge were the beliefs that 'they' lived a long time ago and that 'they' were in some way strange or exotic. This was most clearly illustrated by the way the children reacted to Shiree, the Doll from the Aboriginal Australian family. One child asked 'Why does that Doll have clothes on?' Another was afraid of Shiree and pointed to her, telling the researchers to 'put that Doll away'. Several of the children didn't want to talk about her or look at her, saying that they wanted to play with Tom or Olivia.

Identifying with the Dolls

Prompted by questions from the researchers, the children in this study talked willingly about which of the Dolls looked most like them and the differences they could see between them:

Researcher: Can you notice anything that is different about these Dolls?

Child: That one (Willie) and that one (Shiree) haven't got the same coloured skin.

Researcher Can you tell me what colour their skin is? Do you have some words for that?

Child: Black and a kind of greenish colour.

Researcher: What about the other Dolls, what words would you use for the colour of those Dolls?

Child: That one is white (Olivia) and so is that one (Tom).

The Anglo-Australian children's emphasis on Shiree's skin colour was also associated with uncertainty and discomfort. At times, a few of them actively rejected her. Most often their discomfort and rejection were conveyed through meaningful silences. Some of the children's responses to questions about Shiree were accompanied by a strong verbal or physical refusal to touch or hold her. Sally expressed this simply and powerfully:

Researcher: This one is Shiree. Would you like to hold her?

Sally: No yuck.

Sally had wanted to hold all the other Dolls.

The Vietnamese-Australian children tended to self-identify with Olivia or Tom rather than with Willie. They all remained silent about their reasons except one little girl. She pointed to Willie and said, '... because this one skin most like me'. Yet they commented on skin colour when identifying differences between the Dolls: half of them identified skin and face colour as the first and main difference between them.

MacNaughton compared these self-identification comments and silences about skin tone with the interview with James, a 4 year-old Anglo-Australian child:

Researcher: Well this is Olivia and this is the last of the Dolls you will meet today. Is there anything you can tell me about Olivia?

James: She is very pretty.

Researcher: What makes her pretty?

Researcher: What's that you are pointing at, her dress? Is there anything else that makes her pretty?

James: This does.

Researcher: What's that, can you use your words to tell me?

James: Legs, these are knees.

              [Looks at Olivia's face very closely for several seconds. The researcher picked up on this cue]

Researcher: What about her face, is there anything about her face you can tell me?

James: Her face is lovely like mine because it's lighter. It's like Tom's.

James clearly expressed his opinion about Olivia's loveliness but when asked about Willie he was silent. Like the majority of Anglo-Australian children interviewed he offered no comment on the word Vietnamese. In fact, only two Anglo-Australian children responded to questions about the Vietnamese. One said that Vietnamese people have 'a strange name' and 'shop in markets', the other that they have 'yellow faces and black hair'. MacNaughton notes that layered into Anglo-Australian children's silences about Willie and about being Vietnamese were comments that Willie was 'not Australian'; being Australian meant to them having 'white' skin. The children also said that: 'Willie couldn't be Australian because even though he was born in Australia he is still Vietnamese,' that 'Willie and Shiree are not Australian because they've got different faces,' and 'Willie and Shiree must ask God if they want to be Australian. God might allow Shiree to be Australian but not Willie.'

This is how Kim, a Vietnamese-Australian 4 year old, reacted. The centre that she attends is strongly committed to bilingualism and her teacher believed that Kim spoke sufficient English to participate in the project. Kim held tightly on to Heather's hand when she entered the room. Her attention quickly fixed on the Dolls. She sat down and listened attentively and looked closely at each one as they were introduced to her. Heather explained that she was going to ask Kim some questions:

Heather:	Do you understand, Kim?
Kim:	[Nods]
Heather:	When you look at the Dolls can you tell me which Doll you think looks most like you?
Kim:	[Silence. Looks at Heather then casts her eyes down and points at Olivia. She blushes strongly as she does so.]
Heather:	I see. Can you take a good look for me and be sure.
Kim:	[Nods and then points again at Olivia this time holding Heather's gaze. She blushes again.]

Kim was silent but responded clearly and unambiguously. Her non-verbal communication conveyed that she looked like Olivia (the Doll from a rich Anglo-Australian family) and not like any of the other Dolls. This was particularly interesting given that later in the interview she identified facial and skin tones as the main differences she could see between the Dolls. Her blushes suggest that she knew that the researcher knew that she knew she didn't look like Olivia.

Nearly half of the Australian pre-schoolers in the study saw white skin as normal, lovely, best, and that to them being Australian meant having white skin. They also used whiteness as a category when deciding which Doll looked most like them and when discussing Shiree. One child's only comment during her interview was in response to the question, 'Which Doll looks most like you?' Pointing to Olivia she said, 'I'm White'. MacNaughton claims that the children's reactions to Willie and Shiree are consistent with research by, *inter alia*, Aboud and Doyle (1996). It shows that White children are often negatively biased against Black children.

These are the main things that Macnaughton believes were learned from the project:

■ good organisation and preparation are essential

■ the most powerfully remembered stories and Dolls are those that link with the children's existing knowledge base

■ gender is an important factor in how children attend to and remember the Dolls and their stories

■ children have complex understandings of equity and social diversity issues and can be helped to build respect and learn unfairness through the Dolls and their stories

■ educators and families need to nurture White children's identity and social-emotional development so that they resist false notions of racial superiority and entitlement and grow up willing and able to join ongoing struggles for social justice

■ Persona Dolls and their stories are powerful tools. They excite children's interest, they fascinate adults and they intrigue parents. This provokes conversation and encourages exploration of what children know, how they know it and how we might help them construct fair and equitable meanings about themselves and others

■ we still have much work to do to build a more positive and just world for all. Shiree and her friends and Dolls like them can help us in this work. But it's important to use Persona Dolls with skill and with sensitivity. The process of telling stories to children should be interleaved with the process of listening to them and it must always be done with a spirit of and commitment to fairness and respect for all those involved

It might be useful to reflect on these questions posed by MacNaughton:

- some young children sort people by physical attributes like skin colour rather than by other equally obvious differences of gender or clothes. Why do many not do this?

- what makes physical characteristics such as skin colour that have historically been named as 'racial' so prominent in young children's classifications?

- were the Anglo-Australian children showing racial bias?

- why was Shiree the most rejected Doll and Olivia the only one described as pretty?

Elaine McClement's research

'Persona Dolls in action: an exploration of the use of the Dolls as an anti-discriminatory intervention in the classroom' was the title of the study undertaken by McClement while on a six week block placement at an Educational Psychology Service (EPS). She hoped the following questions would be answered:

- what are the teachers' views of the Dolls?

- what are the children's perceptions of the Dolls?

- how are the Dolls used within the classroom?

- is there a relationship between how the Dolls are used and how well the children relate to the Dolls?

She explains why she decided to use the Dolls:

> The use of Persona Dolls, like any other anti-discrimination intervention, is grounded in the belief that children are not born with attitudes and values but that these are learned and that any learnt prejudice can be unlearned. The underlying conviction is that the unlearning of prejudices will bring about the reduction, or even the elimination, of discrimination and the damaging effects to those who suffer discrimination and those who discriminate. Any intervention which promises to help this process of attitude change is of interest to those who care about equality. The advocators of Persona Dolls have made this claim quite vociferously and Persona Dolls are currently a growing area of interest amongst those who work with early years children. However, there appears to be a limited evidence base to support their use. The question of how we know that they are effective at combating discrimination appears not

to have been satisfactorily answered. On what evidence have the claims about Persona Dolls been based? Who, if anyone, has evaluated the use of these Dolls and how, exactly, has their potential for success been measured?

The infant school in England in which McClement carried out her research had a rich mix of ethnicities and cultures with a large proportion of White British, Caribbean origin and Turkish children. The educators involved in the study were White British and female except for a Turkish female teacher and a Black male teaching assistant.

McClement observed the teachers for approximately forty minutes using the Dolls with children in the nursery, reception and two Year 1 classes. She noted the reactions of the children and gauged their perception of the Doll according to whether they could name it and recall one of its experiences. Children also took part in a child focus group and one-to-one interviews: the Doll used in their classroom was present to keep them focused and to generate information about their perceptions.

The Special Educational Needs Co-ordinator (SENCO) and the teachers completed a questionnaire aimed at discovering what they believed the main purpose of the Dolls to be, how useful they found them, what type of training they had received and what they considered were the benefits and the challenges of using the Dolls.

Teachers' views and children's perceptions

Most of the teachers and the SENCO believed that the main purpose for using the Dolls was to address the issues that were coming up in class in a non-threatening and non-personal way through discussion. When asked about whether the Dolls had been used to tackle racism the SENCO stated that it really wasn't an issue in their school as the population of the school was so mixed anyway. Half of the teachers thought the Dolls were very useful in their work with the children, while one found them to be rarely of use. Only one teacher had received external training in the use of Persona Dolls. The SENCO described how this teacher then borrowed a training video and used it to introduce the Persona Doll approach to the other early years teachers.

Most of the teachers considered working with the Dolls to be quite straightforward but one reported difficulties because she had not kept the Doll's identity constant and another said that some of the children were unfriendly towards the Dolls, occasionally even punching them. The scarcity of Dolls and the cost of buying new ones was commented on. When considering future use, the SENCO said that she would like to get advice on how to introduce the Dolls into key stage 1 and to learn about more effective ways of using the Dolls.

Generally, the children were positive about the Dolls. In interviews they expressed their fondness for their Doll, as the following extract from a group interview with reception children when talking about their Doll Toby illustrates:

Researcher: Can you each tell me how much you liked seeing Toby this year in your class: a little or a lot?

Tala: Very much

Ronda: So much

Lisa: So much

Mhariann: Lots

Jamie: Everyone loves Toby

Researcher: Why?

Jamie: He gives cuddles and kisses and he shakes hands

When asked what they thought the Doll was for and what sorts of things they did with her or him, the children talked about doing stories and said that the Doll talked to them about stealing, road safety and bullying. Many of the children were able to describe the Doll's background or story as if it were another child in their class. When there were two different Dolls, such as a white, blonde and a black, dark-haired Doll, children tended to show a preference for the white, blonde one, as in the case of Micha, a 4 year-old Turkish girl.

Researcher: Do you like both Dolls?

Micha: I like Hannah (the white, blonde Doll)

Researcher: What do you like about her?

Micha: I like the girl with the earrings. I always play with her.

[points to blonde Doll with blue eyes] I like this one.

Researcher: Why do you like her better?

Micha: I don't know.

Micha: She's bigger than her.

              [points to white Doll then the black Doll]

Researcher: How is she bigger?

Micha: She's older

In fact the Dolls were exactly the same height. This conversation, like a number of others, appeared to indicate that children at the ages of 4 and 5 were not only aware of difference but that they also attached value to certain features – as illustrated by Norman, a 4 year-old White boy:

Researcher: Do you have a favourite?

Norman: Yes, one

Norman: I like this one

              [points to the blonde Doll)]

Researcher: Why? Why do you like this one?

Norman: I like her

Researcher: What do you like about her?

Norman: [silence]

Researcher: Can you think of anything about this Doll?

Norman: (no response)

Researcher   Is it her hair or something else?

Norman: (interrupts) I like the hair

Researcher: Yes, the Dolls have different hair. They're quite different
these   Dolls aren't they?

              [silence]

Researcher: They look different. They have different hair. What else is
              different?

Norman: Their T-shirts and their trousers

Despite the children's awareness of differences between the Dolls, several White children like Norman tended to avoid talking about physical differences such as skin colour. Such avoidance was less evident in the responses of Black children, such as Seenat, a 5 year-old African-Caribbean girl.

Researcher:	Can you tell me the name of the Doll you see in class?
Seenat:	Daisy
Researcher:	And what does she look like?
Seenat:	White
Researcher:	And what about her hair colour?
Seenat:	Yellow

Although the Black children interviewed appeared generally more willing to talk about differences in skin colour, the tendency to show a preference for the white Doll remained dominant.

How the Dolls were used and the effect on the children's responses

Some teachers included the Dolls in their weekly plans while others used them whenever an issue arose. The SENCO described how in one class there had been some issues around the children with special needs and that she had used the Doll to help the children discuss what it might feel like not to be accepted. However, it was apparent from the teachers' responses, the classroom observations and from speaking to the children that the Dolls were being used mainly in relation to PSHCE topics, such as stealing and road safety. Children appeared to relate better to their Dolls when their teachers used them in a planned way and during circle time. It seems that the teachers' discomfort with the idea of tackling some forms of discrimination, particularly on grounds of 'race', was reflected by the children, who tended to ignore skin colour when describing the Dolls.

During an observation of a Year 1 class, where a white and a black persona Doll were being used, a White boy expressed his dislike for the black Doll saying that he didn't like 'that Doll' and that he hated her hair. The boy was firmly rebuked by his teacher, reminded that she had already spoken to him about, 'this kind of thing' and told to be quiet. It was apparent that the Dolls, at least in some classes, were not being used to allow children to talk about their beliefs and preferences, particularly concerning race. Lane (1999) emphasises that 'skin colour is very important to children, and adults should never indicate that a child's skin colour doesn't matter'. This simply ignores the reality of racism.

There was also little evidence of the Dolls being used to discuss gender issues.

McClement pointed out that although the school had black Dolls and white, no other skin tones were represented nor was the ethnicity of the school population reflected. All the Dolls were able-bodied and there were more female Dolls than male. In a reception class a teddy bear was used instead of a Doll and when interviewed, the children recalled different names for it and could not remember any time they had used it in class. They appeared disinterested in it and quickly changed the topic of conversation. Similarly, where there had been a change in a Doll's persona, teachers reported that the children became confused and tended to relate less to the Doll.

Lack of training in the use of the Dolls could account in part for the teachers' lack of emphasis on discrimination. Some had no training at all. Issues around difference needed to be recognised and talked about in the classroom. By not initiating this discussion and exploring why children hold certain beliefs and preferences, teachers were not giving children opportunities to think about and challenge their own value judgements. They needed to confront and explore their own feelings of discomfort in talking about difference before they can begin to counter children's discriminatory attitudes and behaviour

McClement suggests that her findings have implications for the Persona Doll anti-discriminatory approach:

- educators need to be committed to tackling discrimination and trained in the use of Persona Dolls if it is to be an effective intervention. They need to be fully aware of what they are doing, why they are doing it and how it should be done

- a whole school commitment to the use of the Dolls must be supported by a corresponding whole school approach to training and staff development

- Dolls need to be selected carefully and with sensitivity

- a suitable area for future research would be the area of teacher perceptions of discrimination amongst children. Perhaps a follow-up study that explores teachers' beliefs would raise some interesting issues whilst helping the teachers to begin to examine their own beliefs

- there are also implications for the role of Educational Psychologists (EPs) in terms of the identification of need, delivery of in-service training and the communication of the purpose and intended use of Persona Dolls. There are extensive possibilities here for future studies that perhaps explore how EPs can support early years settings in delivering effective anti-discriminatory education to children

- although the present study included the perspectives of teachers and children, it failed to take into account the views of parents. This remains a significant gap which could be addressed by a study that considers their views through a parent focus group

McClement maintains that for any early years provision to begin to use Persona Dolls as a tool to help unlearn discrimination, two things must happen. First, the intervention must be properly resourced so that the school has a wide selection of Dolls and, second, funding needs to be ring-fenced to ensure high quality training and ongoing staff development in the use of Persona Dolls and anti-discrimination education generally. Without this the experience of teachers and children in the use of Persona Dolls is restricted and the potential for them to influence children's beliefs is severely limited.

McClement's final thoughts:

We live in a world of growing diversity and therefore both we and our children need more than ever to understand and appreciate difference. There is an abundance of research that supports the view that children develop value judgements and learn to discriminate at a young age and not only on the grounds of 'race'.

Advocators of Persona Dolls, such as Taus, Brown and MacNaughton, assert that prejudices can be unlearned through using the Dolls with children. Any intervention that claims to help tackle prejudice and discrimination in the early stages is, potentially, of great benefit to children and to society and needs to be taken seriously and researched fully.

This case study demonstrates that there are discrepancies between what the teachers' idea of the purpose of Persona Dolls are and what they were originally designed to achieve. The research also revealed the lack of a common understanding about how teachers should be using Persona Dolls and highlighted issues of staff training in the use of the Dolls which has implications for how well children relate to them.

A comparative study of how several schools use the Dolls would be valuable and provide greater generalisation of findings. Perhaps the greatest threat to progress is complacency. In order to challenge discrimination we need to continue to strive to achieve equality for all by reviewing existing policies and exploring new opportunities. This piece of research has gone some way to explore such an opportunity.

Eve Cook's research

This unpublished action research project focused on the introduction of Persona Dolls into seven voluntary and private foundation stage settings in a large English county where one in six people live in sparsely populated rural areas but where there are also several large towns. The population is mainly White and a quarter of the wards are in the 20 per cent most deprived category.

The question Eve Cook hoped to answer was: What are the benefits to educators and children of introducing Persona Dolls into a setting? And what might the disadvantages be? She hoped that involvement in the research would give educators the opportunity to acquire new knowledge and information and, importantly, to use that knowledge to change attitudes, behaviour and practice.

Seven Early Years Development Officers (EYDOs) collected data from seven mainly rural, all White settings across the county. They introduced the Dolls to the children, supported the educators and provided data through their diary sheets. The participants in each setting chose their Doll from a range: male or female, African, African-Caribbean, mixed parentage, European, Chinese, Asian and Romany Traveller.

The EYDOs and educators worked together to build the personas. This entailed thinking about: the Doll's family; where it lived and with whom; language(s); cultural heritage and possibly religion; its likes and dislikes of such things as foods, toys, activities and television programmes. The naming of the Doll was often the point at which the educators first realised they needed to do some research. EYDOs promoted ownership by encouraging them to seek the information they needed, such as about certain cultural and religious backgrounds. Three settings changed the name of their Dolls when they felt it didn't accurately reflect the ethnicity they had decided upon. Terminology, avoiding stereotyping, being aware of their own prejudices were all discussed.

On the first visit the Dolls were brought into the settings by the EYDOs and introduced to the children. The rest of the staff acted as observers, recording their observations on their diary sheets. They were surprised to see how much conversation and interest the visit aroused. Their comments were characterised by adjectives like: excited, interested, concentrating, surprised, intrigued. In all the settings the children looked for similarities between the Dolls' lives and their own. One practitioner said that having the EYDOs leading the first session was a good idea and the fact that the Doll came with her was beneficial because children normally come with someone when they pay their first visit.

Over the next four visits a lead practitioner in each setting worked with the Doll. She and the other educators helped to create stories for the Dolls to tell and continued to observe and note the children's reactions. In some settings discussions about the Doll's skin colour were ongoing. For example, on her second visit to one of these settings the Doll brought a photograph of her mum who was white and her dad who was black. One of the observing educators asked the children who they thought the Doll looked like – a skilful question because it provoked consideration of a range of issues including skin colour.

In another setting, the EYDO noted that when drawing pictures of the Doll after its second visit, one of the children coloured her skin brown, and during the third visit another child remarked that she knew someone at her church with the same name as the Doll's brother. Diary sheets record that one child named his imaginary friend after the Doll's brother and he told everyone that this friend has black hair and black skin that doesn't wash off. Observations showed that educators had introduced the issue of skin colour early on and demonstrated that children were interested and willing to discuss it.

The story told in each setting on the Doll's final visit was based on an incident of discrimination. The lead educators planned the visit with the EYDO and then ran the session. In settings that had Black Dolls the issue was generally around the fact that the children at the Doll's nursery did not want to hold its hand. When the children heard this, they reacted with anger and shock. A child in one of the settings suggested that the solution could be to change her skin colour. In other settings, several diary sheets mentioned that the children had not noticed or commented on the black Doll's colour. One of the lead educators recorded that the children seemed not to care about its colour but the observing educators noted the comments children made about a child with darker skin and a remark that people with different coloured skin live in a different place.

The bullying of the Traveller Doll and the teasing of the Doll who wore glasses were woven into the stories and both these discriminatory issues aroused a good deal of empathy.

The main findings of Eve Cook's research

- both the EYDOs and educators were enthusiastic and willingly undertook research when creating the personas for the Dolls so as to make them accurate and realistic

- the educators were very positive about working with their EYDOs and valued their on-going support and opportunities to discuss what had worked in the sessions and what had not.

Working with their EYDO encouraged some settings to re-evaluate aspects of the persona they had originally created. One educator reported that they had made their Doll less complicated and given it fewer problems

- the EYDOs were also positive about their involvement in the study, as it had given them opportunities to develop their own skills and knowledge and also those of the educators

- their diary sheets beforehand recorded anxieties about how the children would react and about being good role models. Reporting on the day, one EYDO wrote that she absolutely loved it and another said she found it quite a learning curve being in practice again

- educators noted that they had difficulties when sessions were too long or where there were too many children in the group

- children reacted enthusiastically to the Dolls and showed great empathy with them

The diary sheets from all the settings record that they were able to suggest how their Doll might feel and to say what they would have done if they had been present. The strength of their reactions surprised some of the educators. One said she choked at the children's responses and that all the staff present had been moved. Children verbalised their feelings and also used facial gestures and made appropriate sounds. The educators acknowledged the children's emotional engagement with the stories and supported them as they offered strategies and solutions.

■ educators used the Dolls to support the children's learning about cultural diversity, helping them to learn positive attitudes to people who are different from themselves.

The EYDO and the educators in one of the settings created a persona for a Traveller Doll and in the subsequent discussion the children talked about their families and remarked on the differences and similarities in their life-styles.

■ educators found it difficult to appreciate the knowledge and understanding of equality issues the children had already.

On one of his visits the Traveller Doll told the children about how he had been bullied. The diary sheet records that before the session began the lead practitioner was anxious about sharing the incident with the children because she didn't know how far to take it. She noted the children's deep emotional engagement but made no comment on any of the solutions the children suggested. She seemed comfortable sharing cultural information about the Doll but gave the children no opportunities to suggest why the bullies might have behaved in the way they did. Having that conversation could have enabled her to assess what children already knew and understood about Travellers and to address any misconceptions.

■ educators may need more support to use the Dolls to help children unlearn any negative attitudes and behaviour they may already have learned.

One observing practitioner wrote that the subject of name calling should have been discussed further. In another setting the EYDO wondered if the key message might have been diluted or lost for some of the children. The EYDOs used the Dolls at a further session in each of the two settings and re-visited certain aspects of the issue of bullying. They discussed skin colour and name calling with the children again and diary sheets record that the staff were happy for them to do this.

■ an EYDO spoke about the importance of encouraging educators to think about the questions they were considering asking the children in advance of the Doll's visit. Diary sheets showed that several lead educators had done so and were happy to respond to the questions children asked. Children in five of the settings asked whether the Doll was real

- it seems that Persona Dolls have the potential to make a stronger impact in settings where good practice in storytelling exists and there are established circle time routines.

Educators commented on the challenge of storytelling rather than reading aloud. All the lead educators felt they had become more confident in their ability to work with the Dolls by the time they reached the issue session. When information was presented at the right developmental level, the Dolls had more credibility with children so could have greater impact.

- EYDOs, educators and the children all needed time to become comfortable and familiar with their Doll.

Evaluating the project

There were advantages and drawbacks for everyone:

- EYDOs welcomed the opportunity to work with like-minded colleagues on issues they felt were important professionally and personally

Using Persona Dolls provided a focus for the educators' work on equality issues in the various settings. Their close involvement meant that they were able to discuss the children and their reactions to the Dolls and to support educators to plan future sessions, the stories they might tell and the questions they would ask.

- On the negative side, the research was time-consuming. One development officer spent a whole day at Appleby Fair and all spent many hours reading or on the net. Creating the personas provided many challenges

It was important to avoid creating personas that were stereotypical and which reflected the bias and prejudice the Dolls were intended to counter. Diary sheets showed that EYDOs were able to support and guide educators to rethink inappropriate aspects of the persona, but this was not always the case.

- There was little evidence of stereotypical thinking around gender issues being challenged

The educators in one setting noted the negative reaction of some of the older boys to the Doll on the first visit. An observing practitioner wrote that boys thought she was silly and others noted that they didn't like her and said they would have preferred Buzz Lightyear. In another session a child said that he didn't like the Doll because she was a girl. Negative comments were recorded at every visit but none of the sheets recorded the responses to them.

These comments could have provided an opportunity to explore the boys' thinking in more depth. Buzz Lightyear is also a doll – one acknowledged by both adults and peers as a toy that boys are allowed to play with.

■ All the participants in the study were female, which was unavoidable due to the small number of male early years workers in the county but which might have influenced the outcomes

■ All the educators expressed surprise at the children's empathetic and supportive reactions to the Dolls. They often made comments that informed educators of what they already knew and understood about the issues being presented to them but these comments were not always recognised or acted upon.

Eve Cook concluded as follows:

I began this research convinced that working on equality issues with young children was a critically important part of good practice and that good practice did not exist unless it worked within a framework that respects children's rights and develops an understanding of their responsibilities. Young children can learn that we are all unique and our diversity makes us interesting and special. Children have a right to have correct information about the world. And early years educators have a responsibility to value children's cultures and communities and help them recognise unfairness and bias.

I end this study even more convinced of the validity of these beliefs. However, the study shows that working on equality issues with children is complex and demands sustained commitment from all who work with and care about children.

8

A way forward?

I n March 2000 a group of educators had the honour, although they didn't know it, of being the first of many to participate in the innovative, non-threatening Persona Doll training programme. At that time all the training was delivered by Persona Doll trainers who constantly evaluated and reviewed not only their own attitudes and practice but also the content of the training programme. More recently their input, though still substantial, has contracted because through the cascading process some local authorities, colleges and universities now provide their own in-house training modelled on Persona Doll Training's original programme. This anticipated, planned and hoped for development has helped to spread the training and publicise the Persona Doll approach throughout the country and elsewhere. The programme features equality based tasks and discussions around equality issues, working with the Dolls to develop their personas and to create stories around them on anti-discriminatory themes, role-playing and viewing videos and DVDs that show children engaging with and responding to the Dolls and educators' advocation of and commitment to anti-discrimination.

Following on the Persona Doll training that the local authority delivered during 2007, the Equalities Officer in Bradford sent a questionnaire to the educators who had attended the training. The purpose was to assess the value of previous training and the Dolls themselves and to offer any support and further training needed by educators new to the Dolls, or those who were already using them. If further training needs were identified, or if people decided that a network of Persona Dolls users would be useful, these would be pursued.

The Persona Doll Survey in Bradford

[The educators were provided with more space for their answers than is shown here].

1. When did you attend Persona Doll training?

2. Have you bought a doll or adapted a different doll to use as a Persona Doll in your setting?

3. Have you used the Doll in your setting? Yes/No

   If yes, please answer the following questions. (If no go straight to question 12.)

4. Please describe the Doll used.

5. Who has used the Doll? Was it a person attending the training or others in your setting?

6. Please describe in what situations the Doll has been used.

7. How have the children reacted to the Doll?

8. How often has the Doll been used?

9. Are other people in your setting aware of the Dolls and how to use them?

10. Would you or other colleagues find it useful to meet or talk about the Dolls to other people who use the Dolls in different settings?

11. Would you or other colleagues be interested in attending further training or refresher courses? If yes, what would you like the training to cover?

12. If you haven't used a Persona Doll in your setting, could you please try to say why not.

13. Are there any other comments you would like to make regarding the Dolls and/or the training?

The findings

■ thirty eight replies were returned out of 98 questionnaires sent out

■ only three educators want to be involved in a network

■ nine want to take part in a refresher training course; demand is low

- six can't afford to pay for a Persona Doll: this highlights that finance may be an issue

- fourteen managed to buy a Persona Doll or adapt a doll for the purpose

- eighteen used or are using Persona Doll in their settings

- educators showed little interest in developing a network or in attending a refresher training course

- there is a need to look at the content of training itself to identify what needs updating or improving

- there is a need to try running a training session once again for the new educators and those who have expressed interest

- the only way that a Persona Doll network could develop would be: to try to run another course with new participants and bring in those who attended the previous course and are still interested

- the course could be promoted and marketed again

- the training was perceived as being good or excellent

- several people had bought Dolls but not used them

- childminders can't afford to buy Dolls

- many educators are using the Dolls for other purposes than equality and inclusion, such as addressing biting behaviour or a new baby in the family

- Some educators lack confidence in using the Dolls

Certain comments from respondents were revealing:

- our previous manager was not supportive about buying a Doll

- a good tool to use: hope staff feel more confident to use them

- training was one of the most well-presented and enlightening of the courses I have attended.

Issues for the local authority team to consider

- could they support settings with the purchase of Dolls or offer more flexibility about extended loans of Dolls?

■ offering training is expensive if the Dolls are not used afterwards

■ could the training be more flexible? Could less expensive dolls be used?

■ purchasing some Dolls in the near future

The outcome

■ because many of the educators, especially childminders, were attending the training and then not buying and using Dolls, the authority decided to buy a large number of Dolls and offer them at a significantly reduced cost to trainees who attend the full day course. The result is that 100 per cent of trainees now buy and use Persona Dolls after training

■ many educators were reluctant to use the Dolls without further support when they went back to their settings.

To alleviate this, the team offered settings a workshop style session in their own setting. This gives all or most of the educators a chance to know about the Dolls, how to use them and, most important of all, having the opportunity to have a go at introducing an issue to children. These short sessions of one to one and a half hours have gone down really well and are reasonably cost effective.

■ the team have also focused on letting educators get used to using the Dolls with children for quite simple issues so that they gain confidence in using the Dolls before they tackle something more difficult

■ originally they only had one Persona Doll trainer, but now have a pool of staff who can deliver the short workshop style sessions in settings.

Evaluating Anti-discriminatory Practice

This project was set up to consider how the training and the Dolls are enabling local authorities, individual schools, settings, universities and colleges in England to comply with anti-discriminatory legislation and to meet the equality requirements of the QCA at the foundation stage and key stages 1 and 2. Persona Dolls and their stories were not seen as the only way to counter discrimination and promote equality and inclusion. Local authority teams were asked what anti-discriminatory training they organise or facilitate besides Persona Doll training.

Their responses were varied and included:

- information about cultural issues
- how to implement the statutory requirements of the Race Relations Amendment Act
- advice on dealing with and reporting racist incidents
- supporting children learning English as an additional language
- disability awareness
- co-ordinator training relating to special educational needs
- working with asylum-seekers
- race equality issues training for governors

Two questionnaires were piloted. One was sent to foundation stage and key stage 1 and 2 educators, college and university lecturers and the other to members of local authority teams. Audio-taped 45 minute interviews were conducted to probe deeper into areas identified by responses to the questionnaires. The questionnaires and the interviews were designed to encourage people to reflect on their practice, particularly in terms of anti-discrimination.

This trainer summed up what many reported:

> Lots of practitioners know that they need to challenge the prejudices and stereotypes children pick up but aren't sure how to do it and what actual words to use. It is the focus of all our equalities training: we talk about appropriate resources and work through real case studies.

A selection of questions and some of the responses to the questionnaires and interviews are recorded below.

Training and support

An analysis of the data revealed that 88 per cent of people who completed the questionnaire and/or were interviewed were working with children at the foundation stage, 10 per cent at key stage one and 2 per cent at key stage 2.

At interview and through the questionnaire, educators and local authority personnel were asked whether they had received training on how to use Persona Dolls and to identify any aspects of the training they had found particularly helpful.

The majority reported that they had received training and felt they had benefited from it. Working with the Dolls was considered to be the most helpful part of the training, followed by the video extracts, role-play and the awareness raising exercises. In answer to the question about aspects that were not helpful, a few of the educators reported that they found having to role-play embarrassing but no other negative comments were made. A headteacher of a nursery school outlined their training policy:

> All staff in three of the nursery schools in a London borough, including ours, attended a training day and because we had invested that time we also purchased three Dolls. Ever since then as we take on new staff we've tried to get them trained up as soon as possible. We've probably got a couple of members of staff at the moment who haven't received training but we have also got people here who have been using the Dolls for four or five years and so we try to offer a bit of internal training as well as asking one member of staff to model a session for another. The current deputy went off on training when she joined us a couple of years ago and she's very keen on using them.

A number of local authority trainers who provide Persona Doll training mentioned that at the end of the training, participants sometimes say they do not feel confident about using the Dolls. This is important because to use the Dolls effectively requires knowledge, skill, commitment to implementing anti-discriminatory practice and confidence. An Early Years adviser said at interview:

> I think there is a huge difference in confidence among people when they come to training – some are immediately comfortable talking about anti-discrimination and others find it more difficult. ... I don't know if coming on a day will make them feel more confident: in fact sometimes I think it might make them feel less confident, because in a group you will always get those people who speak out, and others might feel 'oh I just couldn't do that'. I think people need a lot more support over time to use them.

Some trainers expressed the opinion that 'it would be much more successful to train settings and schools as a whole, rather than having individuals coming on a course at a centre where they don't know each other'. Local authority teams were asked at interview whether they provide support to participants after training and if so to describe it. The data shows that valuable support is provided by some, others try and arrange regular get-togethers for mutual support and a few give no support at all.

One team wrote that they run a four session in-house programme:

1. the identification of perceived barriers and potential solutions is discussed in groups

2. Cultural Mentors model quality interactions with children using the Dolls

3. the educators in the setting are observed and supported to deliver an inclusive activity

4. a reflective discussion on the activity is held to identify what went well and how it could be improved.

Other teams run on-going informal support and supervision sessions at settings or schools, at which local mentors give lots of examples of families that differ from those of the educators. Sessions are used to boost confidence in developing personas, speaking for the Dolls and addressing equality issues that may not be part of their own personal experience. One educator described the support her setting received from their Early Years mentor during visits over several weeks after the Persona Doll training course that some of the staff had attended:

> Apart from letting us watch her telling a story, she observed each of us and gave suggestions on how we could improve our story-telling technique and develop discussions with the children. This support was particularly helpful because it was offered over time.

Some of the teams felt that the support they provide is inadequate but can't decide how to improve it. Advisors from two North London boroughs tried to develop support networks, but with little success:

> We used to hold a Persona Doll forum every term that provided an opportunity for people who had been on the training to come and discuss any issues. Unfortunately this was very poorly attended and we stopped doing them. Following up on training and the most effective ways to support practitioners afterwards is a theme we discuss a lot as a team. I'm not at all convinced we do it very well at the moment.

Practitioners are very keen after the training but some people need more support to make the best use of the Dolls. We have a follow-up meeting, Persona Dolls Revisited. This is not well attended. It is something we feel needs improving. I think some feel they can't attend if they haven't been able to use the Doll much.

Many of the trainers who completed the questionnaire are trying to adopt a more strategic approach to ensure that the educators who attend the training are supported afterwards to boost their confidence and encourage them to use the Dolls to promote equality and inclusion. They want to avoid the kind of follow up visit where they find educators using the Dolls to reinforce behaviour like, for instance, good sitting or tidying up. This totally disregards the proven opportunities the Dolls offer for dealing with sensitive issues and tackling inequality.

A Kent trainer believes that the follow up support is as important as the training, especially with younger practitioners who lack self-confidence. She runs in-house sessions with the Dolls in which she models bad delivery and asks practitioners to rate on a tick sheet aspects such as voice, body language, vocabulary, tone. She then does it again with good delivery and the practitioners rate the same tick sheet. She finds this goes down well. She added at the end, 'Still working on ways of supporting practitioners and am open to suggestions!'

An Early Years consultant who provides training in the South East pointed out that advisory staff do not always get the time to do the follow up support. She thought this was a pity, as people were very keen when they came on the initial training but not all feel confident enough to work with the Dolls to counter inequality and exclusion.

Raising issues

Educators and members of local authority teams were asked in the questionnaire and at interview to say which of the following issues they raise through the Dolls and to name the three they find the most difficult or challenging to deal with: racism: disability; cultural similarities and differences; sexism; special needs; immigration; homophobia; class; life style eg Gypsies/Travellers; ageism; refugees, other. Analysis of the data revealed that cultural similarities and differences were most frequently talked about followed by racism, life-style, sexism, disability, special needs, refugees. Immigration, homophobia, class and ageism were seldom discussed. Islamophobia was specified as an 'other' by a number of people.

An adviser in Brighton was asked at interview why she had identified racism, homophobia and class on the questionnaire as the issues she found hardest to discuss. She replied:

> Racism because this is what people still find hard to talk about. Homophobia because this is an area that has caused difficulties in the past: we do have a lot of children with same sex parents, but we don't really talk about it in the training. I'm not really sure if it's our brief and I don't think we ever really talk about class. I think with homophobia there are not many stories that I would feel comfortable with: we might tell a story about a child with two mummies or two daddies.

The head of a centre commented:

> There are some issues that are difficult to address anyway, not just through the Dolls – like racist issues, you just have to be very sensitive how you address them. But the Dolls do help because of the range – all colours and ethnicities. But I feel racist issues are difficult.

A practitioner from Dover explained why they haven't tackled sexuality:

> There are now different sorts of partnerships happening within our families that we never had before and they are very open about it. I think it might be difficult to tackle in the group because you don't know what children know about the subject. I suppose we could have a story where a Doll has two mummies.

A college lecturer wrote on the questionnaire: 'Many students in this predominately white area are afraid of addressing racism. They adopt 'the best not to mention it' approach.'

Legislation, the QCA and the Dolls

One question on the questionnaire referred to the fact that the QCA's Curriculum Guidance for the Foundation Stage requires that every child should feel included, respected and valued. Educators were asked if they were using the Dolls to help them meet this requirement and to describe a session. The first two statements are from college lecturers:

> When looking at curriculum issues the Dolls are used to address all areas of difference: we then have a platform to investigate how we can apply anti-

discriminatory practice to the key areas. This is particularly important in the current climate of Islamophobia. For example, I encourage the students to debate topical equality issues such as the burqa: using a Doll with an Islamic background whose mum wears a burqa. Through the Dolls we also confront stereotypes, discuss issues like being Black and British, celebrate languages other than English and address issues around disability by having a Doll who uses a wheelchair.

I think they are a wonderful resource really tapping children's imagination and willingness. Students on Diploma in Child Care and Education courses and Foundation Degree courses have been introduced to the requirement through Social and Emotional Development and Anti-discrimination lectures.

The following comments are from educators working with children at the foundation stage and keystage 1:

We have frequently used our Doll in group time for discussions. All children have an opportunity to speak and to be listened to during these circle times. They have become so successful that staff have asked if we can invest in a second Doll for our nursery.

Empathy for a child who is different, in our case a child with special needs. She is accepted perfectly for who she is within her own class and is considered to be very special. However, it is other children in the school who have not grown up with her who are causing some problems. Even the little girl's cousin is having to deal with comments and questions. So we are working with a Doll in other classes too.

By using the Doll we explored dual heritage and one of the children proudly explained that he was English and Turkish.

Positive responses were given to the question about whether a Persona Doll story sessions had helped a previously reluctant child to join actively in discussions, something which is required by the QCA. Four educators describe their experience:

The child was able to talk about epilepsy in detail. The Persona Doll was embarrassed when she had a fit in the classroom. It enabled him to be the 'expert' on his own medical condition.

The Bangladeshi children were reluctant at first to speak out about their experiences but when I showed them positive ways of sharing their news using the Persona Doll, they were happy to contribute.

When the Persona Doll was introduced the learning support assistant talked about how he was feeling a little sad and lonely because he didn't know anyone yet. A child who tends to keep herself to herself, came up and gave the Doll a hug and said she would be his friend and show him around.

We had a child who has three languages but was not confident speaking in groups. She did on a one to one. During the session with Khalid, our Persona Doll, she spoke to him and told him her name.

The next question referred to the fact that the Every Child Matters outcomes – be healthy, stay safe, enjoy and achieve, make a positive contribution – are less likely to be achieved if children are experiencing or are afraid of verbal and physical abuse, exclusion, name-calling and teasing. Educators who were using Persona Dolls were asked to describe a session in which children could appreciate that abusing, name-calling, excluding and teasing each other was hurtful.

We use the Dolls a lot to discuss friendship issues, bullying and low self-esteem. Our Persona Doll, Kaiya, uses a wheelchair and was told she couldn't dance at the disco. We used lots of Para-Olympic pictures and talked about strong role models like Tanny Grey Thompson, about feelings and what it feels like to be left out.

I told this story. Our Doll, Joel is mixed heritage – African Caribbean/white. He was called names, pushed over and he cut his knee. One of our other Dolls is his friend and wanted to look after him. The children were asked what she could do, who could Joel talk to, how it feels to be called names and who can help?

One of the boys had experienced hurtful comments because he has long hair. One of our Dolls, Taya, has very short hair and is a girl. We used her to initiate a discussion about short and long hair and boys and girls. It was very successful! We all ended up agreeing that you should be able to have what length hair you want and wear what you want.

A question on the Race Relations Amendment Act (2000) pointed out that educators are required to promote good race relations between the children, and asked whether Persona Dolls were helping to do this and to give an example. They seem to have found this more challenging. This is how two teachers and a lecturer responded:

Until recently we were a monocultural setting, 100 per cent Muslim, but now we are getting asylum seekers from parts of Africa, some of whom are

Rastafarians. One of the Asian children, born and bred in Britain, called a little African girl a racist name. We addressed this using a Doll but changed the scenario so as not to pinpoint either child.

In a mostly white school we have a massive mission to talk at length about cultures which differ from our children's and to stress similarities and the realisation that there is no 'normal'. Through the Dolls children meet a much wider range of people than we could possibly invite in and we have wide-ranging discussions. Couldn't do it without the Dolls.

Students use the Dolls to explore how it is possible to promote race relations in positive ways, such as addressing racial taunts and comments through the Doll's stories. I help them develop an understanding of the positive contribution that people of colour have made to British life.

The final question explored whether the process of creating and telling Persona Doll stories helped educators to build their own knowledge, understanding, confidence and ability to encourage children to unlearn any prejudices and stereotypical thinking they may have picked up.

This is what a nursery nurse said:

I have learnt that to promote inclusive practices it is important to have and use positive resources and images, staff who are good role-models, consistency when promoting and challenging the language, attitudes and behaviour of adults and children.

The following responses are from two nursery school teachers:

I've been encouraged to think deeply about the consequences of my actions and attitudes. How making the curriculum more culturally appropriate can help considerably as well as ensuring that fair and just information and resources are available to avoid stereotyping and discrimination. It's important to consider the effects on a child if the clothes their mum wears are not available to dress up in – what message does that give?

The Dolls have broadened the children's horizons and mine.

A primary school teacher had this to say:

From working with the Dolls I am now more skilled in asking questions, more aware of my own attitudes and practices and more able to listen to children and respect their opinions. Having gained in confidence I am not knocked sideways if I make a mistake or I'm not sure how to answer a child's question during a Persona Doll story-telling session.

Lows and highs

During the interviews people were asked to identify the lows and highs they've experienced when using the Dolls. A nursery nurse working in a nursery school in Dover, a primary school teacher in Birmingham and advisers from an inner and an outer London borough all felt that the reluctance of colleagues to use the Dolls was a problem. Their views were echoed by a large number of educators.

> Frustration that members of staff are not using the Dolls more. Some are not comfortable, they find them a bit strange and are embarrassed to be seen talking to a Doll. Some heads and managers don't understand their value and so refuse to buy the Dolls. Encouraging more of them to attend training might be something we will now do.

> When someone comes into the staffroom with a specific problem, I often suggest that it might be a good strategy to use one of our Dolls. But my advice is not heeded. It's a shame because I find they are really effective. Children feel that they can talk freely to the Dolls and that they're being listened to.

> Turnover of staff is a definite low. I visited a setting with three members of staff: two of them were using the Dolls really confidently and one just couldn't or wouldn't. When I visited again sometime later, those two people had left, one of whom was the manager and the Dolls were never used again.

> I suppose the lows are around how much they are used: sometimes I think we have done so much training that everyone would be using them and then I notice that they are all still in the staff room. Some staff never will. But I also feel that we do have strong practitioners who do, so that compensates.

> Our system falls down because once people have attended the training, we don't know whether they are continuing to use the Dolls in the way they were trained to do. We sometimes go into settings and are pleasantly surprised to see that people are using them to talk about equality issues but we don't necessarily get to hear about all the good practice going on. If we could go into settings/schools and do much more modeling, anti-discriminatory practice would be embedded more, but we just don't have time. It is also about creating the persona – you have to do quite a lot of work as a staff to choose a persona and think about the purpose of it and that's quite hard for somebody to go and do, and also whether they get the time to do it with the whole staff is an issue.

From the lows to the highs

Two nursery school teachers describe the highs they experienced:

> I think Persona Dolls are great – I had a little boy with glasses who hated wearing them, but once he realised that Khalid, our Doll was wearing them he was OK. The Doll became almost another child in the nursery and we had such positive feedback. Children do comment on the colour of his skin, especially if we are talking about this and one child said, 'His skin is the same colour as mine'.

> On the positive side, watching the children's faces – they are completely there. Also the amount of language, especially shy ones use and the way children empathise with the Dolls and are able to say, 'that happened to me.'

Three primary school teachers describe their highs:

> When you have used the Dolls once or twice and hear the things children say, you want to keep using them. I also think the Dolls offer a special way of talking through issues with children. Circle time without the Dolls could be fairly nebulous whereas having one sitting there telling the children what happened to her yesterday, provides a focus for the session. We probably wouldn't have the discussions that we have or they would be hard to initiate if we didn't have the Dolls. It's that kind of effect that encourages people to go on using them.

> The children who I had last year and are now in Year 4 with a male teacher keep asking me if the Dolls can visit, but their teacher does not want to use them. I had to cover his class last week and I took in the Dolls. I was slightly concerned because there were two new boys in the class, quite boyish boys and I thought they might turn their noses up at them and laugh. But on the contrary, they were very taken with them and one asked if he could hold a Doll. Maybe it was the enthusiasm of the other children but it shows the appeal of the Dolls even with older children.

> The fact that parents have been so positive. I wrote an article in our school magazine that aroused a lot of interest. We have chatted informally about the Dolls and the children have told their parents all about them.

For two trainers and a lecturer the highs are:

> Practitioners who successfully develop skills in using the Dolls get a huge boost to their own self-confidence and a real sense of achievement. They are pleasantly surprised and delighted by the whole-hearted response of the children.

During sessions we have been surprised and delighted at the way adults empathise and respond to the Dolls, especially those who have had the advantage of previous anti-discriminatory training. As the Persona Doll approach is innovative, practitioners usually show a lot of interest and many report positive effects in terms of their personal development and self-knowledge.

The Dolls help student's to develop empathy, understanding what being a refugee or an asylum seeker entails. Persona Doll work should be part of all degrees, PGCE and childcare courses: then we might see some changes.

Summary of the findings

■ responses to the questionnaire and during the interviews clearly indicate that some educators are reluctant to work with the Dolls to tackle discriminatory issues.

They appear to lack confidence and need more support after training. A number of local authority teams are looking for ways to improve this situation. Developing setting or school based training instead of bringing people together in unfamiliar central venues is a strategy favoured by some. Not having to pay cover would especially help those with a small training budget and would enable more people to be trained. Another effective time and money-saving strategy might be to train and support a cluster of schools.

■ according to the responses on questionnaires and at interviews, participants were well satisfied with the Persona Doll training courses. Many participants go back to their settings or schools and train their colleagues, often with the help of dedicated DVDs and support books

■ however, some trainers expressed frustration.

They complained that even though countering discrimination was the focus of the day and included tasks and discussions to raise awareness of equality issues, when participants were asked to choose an equality issue and weave a Persona Doll story around it, many chose PSHCE type scenarios, such as the feelings of exclusion an older child might experience when a new baby is born. The trainers had hoped the scenarios would deal with social inequality issues.

- a few educators commented on the cost of the Dolls. Persona Doll Training is not in a position to reduce the cost of the Dolls because it is a charity without outside funding, so the training and sales are needed to keep it afloat

Cost came up as an issue during the Bradford research too, particularly because a significant proportion of trainees were childminders. To try and solve the problem Bradford bought a large number of Dolls and now offer them at a significantly reduced cost to trainees who attend the full day course. As reported earlier, almost 100 per cent of trainees now buy and use Dolls after training.

- Islamophobia was not one of the issues respondents were asked about on the questionnaire or when being interviewed. They should have been! Several educators and members of local authority teams added it

- the issues least likely to be addressed through the Dolls were homo-phobia, immigration, ageism and class. This is not surprising since most respondents are working with children at the foundation stage. At key stages 1 and 2 immigration, ageism and class can quite easily be introduced through poetry, stories (including Persona Doll stories), history and citizenship

- there was general consensus among educators. They thought that the Dolls were a valuable tool for exploring issues and helping children to unlearn any prejudiced views they might have learned.

Some expressed their appreciation of the fact that the Dolls can be integrated into the work they are doing around SEAL and Philosophy with the children. At interview and on the questionnaires educators expressed their surprise and delight at the way children empathise and actively support the Dolls when they are unfairly treated or confronted with problems they don't know how to solve:

> Having a Doll makes it easier to discuss issues. If I were just to sit down and do circle time then I think I would find it quite difficult. If I have a Doll as a prop and can say, 'Jeremy feels like this today' it makes it much easier. I can't think of another way of doing it without mentioning actual children's names and making them feel bad. I think these Dolls play a huge part in triggering and sustaining discussions.

Judging by their responses at interview and on the questionnaire, local authority teams consider that the training enables them to provide participants with a non-threatening and enjoyable way to approach anti-discrimination.

> People found the training a practical and helpful way to address anti-discriminatory and culturally appropriate practice. Most people enjoyed developing a persona and a story for their Doll. I think everyone found the training fun, non-threatening and were keen to welcome a Doll into their setting/school and get started.

This sentiment was also expressed in the Bradford research and in many letters of appreciation we receive from local authority teams. These responses were typical:

> This is a very unofficial note to say just how much I enjoyed the Persona Doll training on Wednesday which was definitely the high point of my week. Please pass my appreciation onto the trainers. I've had a quick glance through the course evaluations and they were extremely positive indeed. My aim is to follow up the course with visits to the schools that took part to encourage the purchase of the Dolls and to get the ball rolling. We have several schools where the Dolls have become part of everyday good practice: it needs to be shared with new staff. I am forwarding your contact details to our Gypsy/Traveller Co-ordinator. She is very interested in your providing a course for her key workers.

> I would like to say how well the training was received. Participants were engaged and the evaluation comments were very positive. I think we were all inspired by the course. Hopefully, we can arrange another course and spread the word further. After all the media coverage of migrant workers, areas like ours are facing greater challenges when we combat racism and prejudice. I believe Persona Dolls are a wonderful resource for schools that take on this work.

Many educators are motivated by children's spontaneous and whole-hearted responses to develop their work with the Dolls. This view was expressed on many questionnaires and at interviews. It is reasonable to conclude that given training and support to boost their confidence and equip them with the skills and knowledge they need, educators are generally able, willing and happy to work with the Persona Dolls at circle time to promote PSHCE. Having to deal with anti-discriminatory issues is more of a problem but those who are successfully using the Dolls for this purpose seem well-satisfied with the results:

The Dolls enable me to provide enjoyable learning experiences that build on children's sense of identity, self-esteem and confidence and encourage them to respond to others with empathy, respect and sensitivity.

This typical comment chimes with the thinking of Selleck and Griffin (1996:169):

We need the vision to plan for whole human beings who have a clear and realistic personal identity whatever combination of cultural or religious background, racial origins, gender, ability or disability that may be. ... Children who can collaborate and learn together in harmony with other people are likely to respect and value differences. Children who are able to have intimate responsive relationships with their significant adult will have better access to relevant learning experiences. Children who play in inspirational safe and challenging environments will take these values into adulthood and pass them onto future generations. An ethos of respect and dignity in childhood may be set from the cradle to the grave.

9

The struggle continues

The research outlined in this book confirms previous findings and validates the potential of the Persona Dolls to challenge inequality. It also raises the $64,000,000 question: why despite equality legislation and all the statutory and non-statutory requirements, is anti-discriminatory education still the exception and not the rule?

The Australian Preschool Equity and Social Diversity research project led by Professor Glenda MacNaughton, Elaine McClement's school based research and Eve Cook's action research, all summarised in chapter 7, highlight the well-established fact that children learn discriminatory attitudes and behaviour from the world around them. All three researchers stress that to combat this learning effectively educators need training, commitment, confidence, skill and sensitivity. Only then can they utilise the full power of Persona Dolls to promote anti-discriminatory education.

Bradford provides a model. It has successfully changed the way training and support are organised. Settings are provided with workshop style sessions that are inexpensive to run and give all or most of the educators a chance to know about the Dolls, how to use them and, most importantly of all, give them an opportunity to try to introduce an anti-discriminatory issue through the medium of a Persona Doll. Bradford encourages educators to use the Dolls to talk about straightforward topics at first and so gain confidence before tackling issues of discrimination.

Even though the law and the QCA require it, not all educators are en-suring that equality and inclusion characterise their practice. There are some who seem reluctant to put their toe in the water, others who are trying but are held back by their own lack of knowledge, awareness and confidence and yet others who are going full steam ahead. Awareness is the first step on the ladder to change. From early childhood most of us begin absorbing many of the prejudices and stereotypical thinking so deeply rooted in the history of this country. As adults we have the capacity to reflect on our attitudes and a responsibility to counter the detrimental effects of prejudice and discrimination on children's lives. This includes knowing not only about which groups in our society are the targets of prejudice and discrimination but also appreciating the extent to which the lives and education of children are affected by racism, poverty and class, sexism and gender identity. A good place to start is with racism. Louise Derman-Sparks (1998) explains it this way:

> Our work takes place within a social-political context and history of systemic racism and other forms of oppression. We begin with racism as our starting point for change and then make the connections with the other primary oppressions in our society (sexism, classism, ableism, heterosexism, and so on). ... We begin with racism because it is not possible to build a just, multi-ethnic community or to work in culturally relevant ways on any issues unless we do so.

Racism needs to be understood not just as a matter of individual pre-judice and discriminatory practice but as an institutionalised force that advantages those who are defined as White and disadvantages those defined as not White. To combat racial injustice actively it is important that those of us who are White know about our colonial past and also understand the role that White privilege and power play in bolstering and sustaining racism. Mathias and French (1996) quote the words of a woman on recognising the implications of being White:

> As a White person, I was taught to see racism only in individual acts of mean-ness, not in invisible systems conferring dominance on my racial group. I think Whites are carefully taught not to recognise White privilege, as males are taught not to recognise male privilege. I have come to see White privilege as an invisible package of unearned assets which I can count on cashing in each day ... Whites are taught to think of their lives as morally neutral, norma-tive, average and also ideal, so that when we work to benefit others, this is seen as work which will allow them to be more like 'us'.

MacNaughton (2007) has told the story she calls, 'Kim's Blushes' (see in chapter 7) to many audiences in Australia, the UK, New Zealand and Singapore. To all of them she posed the questions: 'Why did Kim make the choice she did and why did she blush when making this choice?'

The responses she received from White colleagues in these countries included:

- have you considered that it's impossible to answer the questions without more information about Kim, her background, her language skills, etc.?

- could you have framed the research questions in ways that confused or were misleading?

- did Kim think that that is how she looked because she doesn't see skin colour as an issue?

- did Kim just want to go to the toilet or go out and play?

- aren't you making a lot out of something that wasn't really that important?

Black colleagues gave quite different responses:

- I could feel my skin creep as you told Kim's story – I just knew what she felt (Indigenous Hawaiian woman)

- I felt I wanted to cry because I knew those blushes well. (Japanese woman)

- very powerful. I am truly emotional, feeling a bit teary eyed and choked up (Indian-American woman)

- I know how Kim felt. When I was 4 years old I asked my mother to wash my skin so that the colour would come off. I was the only dark skinned child in my kindergarten. I want to thank you for telling Kim's story. It is important that people know how it feels (Indian Australian woman)

- Kim's story is very true for me. I always wanted white skin (Malaysian Australian woman)

- you have just told the story of my sisters. My wife and I have been close to tears as you talked but you have said what needed to be said (Indigenous Australian man)

There followed a long discussion about how his sisters had spent their lives trying to pass as White and the tragic implication of their sense of being unable to 'pass', leading to drug abuse and suicide.

MacNaughton summed up her own reactions:

> Through Kim and other children and adults, I have learnt that whiteness matters in the lives of each one of us; that it matters differently depending on our relationship to it and its injustices. ... Those who experience racial injustice, people of colour across national borders, point to the intimate connections between skin colour, experience, desire, and emotion in their responses to Kim's Blushes. ... I am drawn to know that race matters to young children, I am drawn to ask, 'What must we do in early childhood to make racial justice matter? And I am drawn to question, 'How can we create racially just White identities in our work with children?' ... These are challenging questions but to ignore them is to make racism and the whiteness it sits upon live on in our lives and in the lives of young children.

Beth Scott (2008) wrote this poem when she was still in primary school:

Racism

Our world goes round
Time passes by
But our minds don't change
I wonder why?
We still think that different is wrong
They say it is in the past
And that it is all gone
But as I look upon our world
I see not happiness but fear
Upon the victims of Racism!

Islamophobia

The dramatic rise of Islamophobia may explain why anti-discrimination is still not flavour of the month. 9/11, the London bombings and the 'war on terror' didn't create Islamophobia but they have certainly sharpened and intensified it and have focused the attention of the government, the media and the public on what it means to be British and on issues of national cohesion. This has led to attacks on multiculturalism and on Muslim communities, further heightening Islamophobia. Initially multiculturalism emerged as a concession to the agitation for equality from Black communities and the antiracist movement. It was about integration – but integration requires a society in which everyone can feel they belong which is patently not the case. Sivanandan (*Guardian* 3.9.2006) explains:

> Integration provides for the coexistence of minority cultures with the majority culture ... the aim of integration is a multicultural, pluralistic society. ... It is only in combating racism that multiculturalism becomes progressive. The fight for multiculturalism and the fight against racism go hand-in-hand; antiracism is the element that makes multiculturalism dynamic and progressive.

The Communities Secretary, the head of the Commission for Equality and Human Rights (CEHR) and the leader of the Conservative Party all argue against multiculturalism from a different standpoint. They question its value on the grounds that it encourages separateness rather than integration.

Launching the government's Commission for Integration and Cohesion in August 2006 the Communities Secretary said:

> ... for some communities in particular, we need to acknowledge that life in Britain has started to feel markedly different since the attacks on 9/11 in New York and 7/7 in London ... And as this complex picture evolves, there are white Britons who do not feel comfortable with change. They see the shops and restaurants in their town centres changing. They see their neighbourhoods becoming more diverse. Detached from the benefits of those changes, they begin to believe the stories about ethnic minorities getting special treatment, and to develop a resentment, a sense of grievance.

> The issues become a catalyst for a debate about who we are and what we are as a country. About what it means to live in a town where the faces you see on the way to the supermarket have changed and may be constantly changing.

> I believe this is why we have moved from a period of uniform consensus on the value of multiculturalism, to one where we can encourage that debate by questioning whether it is encouraging separateness.

The emphasis on separateness as a problem threatening the cohesion of the country is not new. From the 1880s when Jewish people came to Britain seeking sanctuary from persecution in Eastern Europe, they were perceived as a threat to the British way of life and blamed for not integrating, for their separateness, their strangeness. Maleiha Malki wrote in the *Guardian* (2.2.2007):

> As believers in one God they were devoted to their holy book which contained strict religious laws, harsh penalties and gender inequality. Some of them established separate religious courts. The men wore dark clothes and

had long beards and the women covered their hair and a royal commission warned of the dangers of self-segregation. ... Some Jews were anarchists and a few resorted to violent attacks such as the bombing of Greenwich Observatory in 1894 – described at the time as an 'international terrorist outrage.'

Today the finger of blame has moved on. It is now pointing inexorably at Muslims, who are being portrayed as the dangerous fifth column, vilified in the media as terrorists and treated as the Trojan horse in the heart of British society. This prompted Martin Jacques, a visiting research fellow at the Asia Research Centre, London School of Economics, to ask the apposite question:

And what is to blame for this failure to integrate? Prejudice, perhaps? Discrimination? Racism? No. According to David Cameron, Ruth Kelly and many others, the cause would appear to be multiculturalism. ... The attack on multiculturalism is the thin end of the racism wedge. It seeks to narrow the acceptable boundaries of difference at a time when Britain is becoming ever more diverse and heterogeneous. ... Antipathy towards Muslims, meanwhile, threatens to roll back hard-fought antiracist gains, which, over the decades, have won a degree of respect for ethnic minorities and an acceptance of the principle of difference. These gains have always been fragile. Important ground is now being ceded as Islamophobia becomes the acceptable face of racism and the attack on multiculturalism finds important new recruits.

The impact on race relations of the wars in Afghanistan and Iraq has been devastating. Fear, suspicion, hostility and resentment have accelerated alarmingly. In towns like Bradford and Oldham, White children who should be attending the 90 per cent Asian schools are at the 90 per cent White schools up the road. Research by the University of Lancaster shows that these children were less willing to integrate than Asian children of a similar age. Settings and schools are required to work towards community cohesion but under conditions like these it becomes more difficult to achieve. As Ros Garside (*Race Equality Teaching*, 2007) says:

Community cohesion is defined as being about working towards a society in which there is a common vision and sense of belonging for all communities, the diversity of people's background is appreciated and valued, similar life opportunities are available to all and strong and positive relationships exist and are developed in the workplace, schools and the wider community. Sadly, institutions which live out these values are not the norm and disturbingly the CRE has recently named schools as being the least effective public organisations in terms of delivering the Race Relations Amendment Act.

A more optimistic note is struck by educators involved in the Linking Schools Scheme. They believe that the scheme is helping to build a more cohesive society by bringing children from communities estranged from one another, closer together. In Oldham for example, a Church of England school with an almost 100 per cent Muslim student body is linked with a primary school with almost 100 per cent White children. The children regularly share daily lessons on national curriculum subjects, visit various places of worship, go to the theatre and concerts together and participate in a range of shared sporting activities. In situations like this, Persona Dolls have an important part to play in strengthening bonds of friendship, mutual understanding and awareness. A children's centre in Bradford has integrated the Dolls into the curriculum for some years now and has incorporated them into their anti-discriminatory practice.

The underpinning philosophy of the Linking Schools Scheme is that society cannot be sustainable if some parts live in ignorance and don't try to get on with the other parts. It seems reasonable to assume that if this rationale were broadened to include providing adequate housing, raising the standard of living and life chances of Black people and White who are presently living in poverty, then racism and feelings of alienation would decrease. This in turn would undermine support for organisations like the British National Party and foster greater social cohesion.

A hard nut to crack

Deeply held discriminatory beliefs perpetuate inequality and act as a barrier to change. And these are themselves hard to change. Negative attitudes towards particular groups of people may be so strongly held that the idea of changing them is not even contemplated.

This can apply to homophobia. It is based on the widely held belief that heterosexuality, the emotional and sexual relationships between men and women, is normal and that homosexuality, the emotional and sexual relationships between people of the same sex, is abnormal and unnatural. This attitude was clearly evident on March 3 2004 at the picket of the premises where nursery teachers were being trained to work with Persona Dolls. The protesters made such a noise shouting, 'Babette Brown go home' (I wasn't there!) that the police had to be called. The Parent Truth Campaign organised the picket. Their graphic

141

posters later appeared on their website claiming that: 'specially made dolls are being used to promote homosexuality to children as young as three' and that 'there is an underlying agenda to push gay relationships'. Mrs Willis, a mother of five and a member of the group was quoted as saying:

> We encourage parents to demand that these Dolls are never used in the classroom and that those responsible for this bizarre idea are called to account and sacked. After the repeal of Section 28 we were promised that there would be no promotion of homosexuality in our schools. Today, we have a clear example of nursery children being indoctrinated to accept perverse and immoral life styles. It is a demonstration of how far the 'gay' lobby have infiltrated the educational system and the local authority and their executives are actively encouraging it. The Dolls are given a 'persona' such as the daughter of a lesbian parent and children are forced to cuddle the Doll and accept the special home circumstances surrounding it. This is brain-washing worthy of communist China where children's minds were 'bent' to accept the norms of the 'Cultural Revolution' and encouraged to denounce parents.

The Council in their reply re-affirmed their support for the Dolls. Their spokesperson said:

> The Dolls, which are used elsewhere in the UK and the USA, are useful tools in combating discrimination, including racial and religious prejudice and disability, helping youngsters learn to respect other children's feelings and family structures... The training day provided early years professionals with the opportunity to work with Persona Dolls alongside trainers to discover their potential for exploring and confronting equality issues with young children. The ordinary soft Dolls reflect different ethnic groups and can be used to explore gender, behaviour and disability issues. They are not used to explore issues relating to sexual health or part of any sex education programme. The only thing that defines their gender is their clothing.

The Children's Minister has strongly condemned anti-gay bullying and the casual use of homophobic language in schools. Addressing Stonewall's annual Education for All conference in 2006 he said:

> We need to make sure that every teacher has the knowledge, skills and confidence to deal with incidents of homophobic bullying. To challenge intolerance and disrespect in whatever form it rears its ugly head. Just as it took several years for racial equality laws to feed into real culture change

where racist language became unacceptable, so we now need to achieve the same with homophobic language. We aren't there yet. Just one example is the casual use of homophobic language. This is too often seen as harmless banter instead of the offensive insult that it really represents.

Homophobia is not always included in anti-bullying and equal opportunities policies even though it is clearly connected with bullying. Terms like 'gay', 'a poof' or a 'lezzie' are being used in primary schools to wound and abuse. Children in gay and lesbian families need to see their family set-up represented and respected, and children from more traditional families may need encouragement to accept that there are different ways of living in families and learn that it's wrong and hurtful to harass their peers whose family structure is different from theirs. Telling stories around Persona Dolls living with their two mums or two dads would seem to be an accessible, engaging and non-threatening way to respond. By talking about the suffering that homophobia generates, children can begin to understand that it is unfair, hurtful and can have serious consequences.

Educators may be unaware that they have gay colleagues or children from gay or lesbian families who are keeping their relationship secret because of homophobia. Parents may feel that they will be disapproved of, talked about and laughed at behind their backs and, more seriously, may worry about possible repercussions on their children. Educators may not know that according to figures from the Teacher Support Network, two thirds of gay teachers and lecturers have experienced harassment and discrimination at work. Yet legislation in force since December 2003 makes it unlawful to discriminate directly or indirectly or to harass or victimise anyone because of their actual or perceived sexual orientation. Not everyone knows that in Nazi Germany homosexuals were forced to wear a pink triangle and that 10,000 were exterminated simply because of their sexual orientation.

The media

The media and particularly the tabloids crucially influence attitudes. Political correctness, or rather the deliberate misinterpretation of the concept by some journalists, is I believe partly responsible for the apparent unwillingness of many educators to address issues of discrimination. The term was initially introduced to encourage the sensitive use of words so as to value and respect people. However, in the 1980s, the media's ridicule and undermining gave rise to the belief that certain terms were not 'pc' on the grounds that they were offensive to Black people. For example, 'you must not ask for black tea or coffee but for tea or coffee without milk' and 'you should not refer to the black-board or to black bags'. This sending up by the media continues to create and sustain a pervasive, insidious and mocking attitude among the general public. It nourishes the fear of saying the wrong thing, being accused of being racist and opening a can of worms. The outcome is that many people mouth what they think they are supposed to say without necessarily understanding or believing it.

According to Newstead (2006):

> Fear about not getting it right, fear of offending someone ... And the fear stops us thinking – it stops us paying attention to what we're actually trying to achieve, it stops us questioning the logic of what we're actually doing ... Just like all the other parts of our professional practice, it is a process on which we need to reflect.

It may be that the media hype about bogus asylum seekers, benefit spongers and disability frauds has fed the perception that far from being discriminated against, these undeserving people are getting preferential treatment.

Education policies and their impact on anti-discriminatory education

Prime Ministers Thatcher and Major were both strongly opposed to egalitarian practice because they believed it led to a general decline in standards. Teacher training colleges were a particular target. They were harshly criticised for advocating collaborative learning, anti-racism, democratic classrooms and the democratic management of schools.

This attitude is summed up in John Major's speech at the Conservative Party Conference in 1992, quoted here by Hill and Cole (2001:20):

> When it comes to education, my critics say I'm 'old fashioned'. Old fashioned? Reading and writing? Old fashioned? Spelling and sums? Great literature, and standard English grammar? Old fashioned? Tests and tables? British history? A proper grounding in science? Discipline and self-respect? Old fashioned? I also want reform of teacher training. Let us return to basic

subject teaching, not courses in the theory of education. Primary educators should learn to teach children how to read, not waste their time on the politics of race, gender and class.

Claire and Holden (2007) point out that teacher training courses also carry some of the responsibility. They cite a number of studies. In their survey of 187 primary and secondary ITE students in Wales, Robbins *et al* (2003) showed that two thirds did not feel qualified to talk to children about controversial issues. The students Revell (2005) interviewed considered their training to be apolitical, 'overwhelmingly practical, concentrating on curriculum delivery' and not requiring them to understand or question underlying issues. Hess (2004) found that teachers were anxious about tackling politically charged issues and afraid they would be accused of indoctrination. They felt that they did not have sufficient education and training to deal with controversy.

These findings are not surprising considering that opportunities for critical thinking and reflection have been almost completely pushed out of the curriculum. This process has been worsened by the introduction of three year and even shorter teaching courses.

It is heartening to see that so much in the EYFS accords with anti-discriminatory principles. However, in article after article devoted to detailed discussions of the framework, few, if any, of the authors talk about equality and inclusion although these are key concepts threaded through the EYFS. When commenting at the consultation stage, the CRE had this to say:

> [We] welcome the focus throughout the document on the key role of the EYFS in improving the life chances of all children. We strongly support the consistent underlying themes of ensuring that the individual needs of all children are met and that no child is excluded or disadvantaged because of ethnicity, culture or religion, home language or family background. We are also encouraged by the requirement that providers promote equality of opportunity and anti-discriminatory practice.

> Although not all early years settings are covered by the statutory requirement of the Race Relations Act 1976, as amended, the CRE would expect all settings to comply with the principles of the Act by putting race equality at the centre of their work.

Ofsted's role

There does not seem to be much attention paid to equality issues during inspections. Ofsted reports seldom include comments on either the settings or schools who make equality and inclusion a priority or those that pay little attention to these issues. If equality is not considered important enough to be mentioned then educators may be getting the message that it doesn't really matter if they are failing to implement the QCA equality requirements. This impression is unlikely to move anti-discrimination to the fore and may go some way to explain why so many educators are using the Dolls for PSHCE and not the anti-discrimination purposes for which they were primarily developed.

Ofsted's revised *Race Equality Scheme* (2006) proposes that an equality impact assessment be carried out on existing policies, practices and procedures, to identify where action needs to be taken to make improvements or to devise new policies to promote equal opportunity and take into account the needs of children with diverse needs during inspection or regulation work. Race equality is central to policy-making, service delivery and employment practices, as well as to their inspection, regulation and enforcement responsibilities. This focus embraces learners, children, young people and employees of all backgrounds – all steps in the right direction. But this scheme was introduced in 2006 and not much appears to have changed. How seriously Ofsted inspectors will incorporate into their assessment the Race Relations Amendment Act, the equality requirements of QCA and initiatives like EYFS, SEAL and KEEP is crucial. This raises certain questions:

- will the present focus during inspections in settings and schools on literacy, numeracy and other academic subjects be extended to include how equality issues are dealt with?

- will failure to meet equality requirements incur comparable censure to academic failure?

- will all inspectors receive adequate in-depth specific training on racism and other equality issues to enable them to inspect and report on them?

- will the degree to which race equality issues appear in reports depend solely upon the sensitivity and understanding of individual inspectors?

■ is this huge bureaucracy with its wide-ranging responsibilities really able to act effectively as an equalities watchdog?

■ are racial equality, equal opportunities and anti-discriminatory education recognised by all at Ofsted as central features of educational inclusion and a key principle underpinning the National Standards?

The findings of the reports *Race Equality in Further Education* and *Race Equality in Education* are encouraging. The majority of colleges inspected are meeting their responsibilities under the Race Relations Amendment Act 2000 and race equality issues are a strong feature of the National Curriculum. Welcoming them, Ofsted's Director of Education said:

> Today's reports show what can be achieved when race issues are an integral part of the school and college curriculum. Teachers in the schools and colleges we visited said they are pleased that race issues are no longer simply a 'bolt-on' to the curriculum. There is still work to be done but the signs are good. Children and young people need a chance to question, discuss and debate what can sometimes be difficult and contentious issues when they are at school or college.

However, in the 2005-2007 Monitoring and Enforcement Plan report of the newly formed *Commission for Equality and Human Rights* Ofsted is cited as 'arguably the most uncooperative public authority the Commission for Racial Equality had to deal with over the last two years'. In its defence, an Ofsted spokesperson drew attention to the fact that in September 2007 its guidance to inspectors was strengthened and that further training on race equality is planned. Ofsted childcare and early education inspectors were involved in EYFS Underpinning Knowledge training in 2007/2008, in which equality issues were emphasised.

The impact of the training on Ofsted inspections and their reports is eagerly awaited.

Taking action

Changing attitudes and behaviour is vital but will not by itself stop the rising tide of racism and social inequality. The education system itself reproduces inequalities: the most affluent are able to send their children to private schools and the top universities from which most step into highly paid professional and managerial jobs, so maintaining the process whereby the rich stay rich.

Britain is the fourth richest country in the world, yet almost three million children are living in poverty. The London Borough of Hackney is one of the poorest places in western Europe: a quarter of homes have no bathroom or toilet and two thirds of primary school pupils, the highest number in the country, qualify for free meals.

Closing the gap between the groups who are succeeding academically and those who are falling behind requires structural changes as well as policies and practices based on anti-discriminatory principles. According to research funded by the Sutton Trust in 2007, the brightest 7 year old children in Britain's poorest homes are outperformed by the least able 7 year olds from wealthy homes. It concluded that social class is still the biggest predictor of educational achievement, suggesting that the advantages of being born in a privileged home have not changed in 30 years: social mobility is at a standstill. As Nelson Mandela said when he became an Amnesty International ambassador of conscience in 2006:

> ... as long as injustice and inequality persist in our world, none of us can truly rest. We must become stronger still. ... It is my wish that this award should help all activists around the world to shine their candles of hope for the forgotten prisoners of poverty. Like slavery and apartheid, poverty is not natural. It is people who have made poverty and tolerate poverty, and it is people who will overcome it.

Economic, political and social factors are all part of the problem – and of the solution. Many organisations, among them the Refugee Council, the National Children's Bureau, Jcore, the Daycare Trust, the Child Poverty Group, and various Gypsy/Traveller and disability organisations constantly campaign to try and make Britain a more equal society. Countless numbers of committed people all over the country are helping to improve the lives and life chances of those who are disadvantaged. And, crucially, there are the disadvantaged who strongly demand and fight for their rights. Struggling against injustice and oppression is difficult, emotionally draining and isolating. We have a responsibility and the power to work actively towards transforming society and to keep the vision alive – that one day all children will grow up free from racism, sexism and the other social inequalities. James Baldwin was right when he said: 'Not everything that is faced can be changed, but nothing can be changed until it is faced.'

Inspiring words from Robin Richardson (2007:11) to end with:

> Reducing and removing inequalities involves challenging attitudes, yes, most certainly. But there's more, much more, to the equalities agenda than that. For example, if we wish to challenge the stereotype of Other as weak and resourceless, the need is not primarily to educate ourselves about the Other but actually to share resources with the Other, empower the Other and (it follows) disempower ourselves.

And a message of hope from the poet, Arthur Hugh Clough:

Say not the struggle naught availeth

Say not the struggle naught availeth,
    The labour and the wounds are vain,
The enemy faints not, nor faileth,
    And as things have been they remain.
If hopes were dupes, fears may be liars;
    It may be, in yon smoke conceal'd,
Your comrades chase e'en now the fliers,
    And, but for you, possess the field.
For while the tired waves, vainly breaking,
    Seem here no painful inch to gain,
Far back, through creeks and inlets making,
    Comes silent, flooding in, the main.
And not by eastern windows only,
    When daylight comes, comes in the light;
In front the sun climbs slow, how slowly!
    But westward, look, the land is bright!

Bibliography

Abbott, L and Nutbrown, C (eds) (2001) *Experiencing Reggio Emilia*. Philadelphia: Open University Press.

Aboud, F (1988) *Children and prejudice*. Oxford: Basil Blackwell.

Aboud, F and Doyle, A (1996) 'Does talk of race foster prejudice or tolerance in children?' in *Canadian Journal of Behavioural Science* 28 (3).

Adonis, A and Pollard, S (1997) *A Class Act, the Myth of Britain's Classless Society*. Hamish Hamilton: London.

Bertram, T (2007) 'Raise your game' in *Nursery World* 7 June.

Bisson, J (1997) *Celebrate: an Anti-Bias Guide to Enjoying Holidays*. St Paul: Redleaf.

Bolloten, B (ed.) (2003) *Home from Home – a guidance and resource pack for the welcome and inclusion of refugee children and families in school*. London: Save the Children

Bradman, T and Browne, E (1986) *Through my Window*. New Jersey: Silver Burdett.

Brooker, L (2002) *Starting school: young children learning cultures*. Buckingham: Open University Press.

Brooker, L (2005) Cultural Diversity and Early Years Ideology, in N. Yelland (ed.) *Critical Issues in Early Childhood Education*. Berkshire: Open University Press.

Brown, B (1994) 'Thinking it Over: the terminology of 'race" in *Multicultural Teaching* 12 (2).

Brown, B (1995) 'Whom Do We Include: do Irish and Jewish people suffer racism?' in *Nursery World* January.

Brown, B (1998) *Unlearning Discrimination in the Early Years*. Stoke-on-Trent: Trentham Books.

Brown, B (2001) *Combating Discrimination*. Stoke-on-Trent: Trentham Books.

Brown, C, Barnfield, J and Stone, M (1990) *A Spanner in the Works*. Stoke-on-Trent: Trentham Books.

Burgess-Macey, C and Crichlow, K (1996) The Equal Opportunities Curriculum, in Claire, H and Holden, C (2007) *The Challenge of Teaching Controversial Issues*. Stoke-on-Trent: Trentham Books.

Cannella, G (1998) *Deconstructing Early Childhood Education: Social Justice and Revolution.* New York: Peter Lang Publishing.

Children Act (2004). London: HMSO.

Coard, B (1971) *How the West Indian Child is made Educationally Subnormal in the British School System.* London: New Beacon Books.

Connolly, P (1998) *Racism, gender identities and young children, Social relations in a multi-ethnic inner-city primary school.* London: Routledge.

Cook, E (2004) 'What are the benefits to practitioners and to children of introducing Persona Dolls into a setting?' Unpublished dissertation.

Cousins, J (1999) *Listening to four year olds: how they help us plan their education and care.* London: National Children's Bureau.

Dau, E (1996) Exploring Families: the diversity and the issues, in B. Creasner and E. Dau (eds) *The Anti-Bias Approach in Early Childhood.* Sydney: Harper Educational.

Davies, B (1993) Shards of Glass. *Children reading and writing beyond gendered identities.* New Jersey: Hampton Press.

Derman-Sparks, L and the ABC Task Force (1989) *Anti-Bias Curriculum: tools for empowering young children.* Washington DC: National Association for the Education of Young Children.

Derman-Sparks, L (1998) Overview of the Culturally Relevant Anti-Bias (CRAB) Leadership Project in S. Cronin, S., L. Derman-Sparks *et al* (eds) *Future Vision Present Work.* St. Paul: Redleaf Press.

Derman-Sparks, L and Brunson-Phillips, C (1997) *Teaching/Learning Anti-Racism: a developmental approach.* New York: Teachers College Press.

DfES (2001) *Code of Practice on the Identification and Assessment of Children with Special Educational Needs.* London: HMSO.

DfES (2003) *Exploring the Field of Listening to and Consulting with Young Children* (DfES Research Report 445). London: DfES.

DfES (2004) *Aiming high: Guidance on supporting the education of asylum-seeking and refugee children.*

Dowling, M (2008) 'With Good Reason' in *Nursery World* 21 February.

Epstein, D (1993) *Changing Classroom Cultures: anti-racism, politics and schools.* Stoke-on-Trent: Trentham.

Faragher, J and MacNaughton, G (1990) *Working with Young Children.* Collingwood: TAFE.

Farmer, N (2008) 'Boy zone in London' *Nursery World* 17 January.

Freire, P (1994) *Pedagogy of Hope: Reliving Pedagogy of the Oppressed.* London: Continuum.

Fullan, M (1991) *The New Meaning of Educational Change.* Cassell: London.

Gaine, C (1987) *No Problem Here.* Hutchinson: London.

Gaine, C (1992) Why We Need an Anti-Racist Approach In Mainly White Areas, in Garside, R (2007) 'News and Comment' in *Race Equality Teaching* 25 (3).

Geras, A (2005) *A Candle in the Dark*. London: A&C Black.

Ginnis, S and Ginnis, P (2006) *Covering the Curriculum with Stories: six cross-curricular projects that teach literacy and thinking through dramatic play*. Carmarthen: Crown House.

Griffin, S (2008) *Inclusion, Equality and Diversity in Working with Children – from good intentions to effective practice*. Oxford: Heinemann.

Gussin Paley, V (1984) *Boys and Girls: Superheroes in the Doll Corner*. London: University of Chicago Press.

Hill, D and Cole, M (2001) *Schooling and Equality*. London: Kogan Page.

Holland, P (2008) 'An expert's view' in *Nursery World* 24 January.

Houston, G *Mixed Race, not Mixed up: Supporting Children from Multi Racial Families in Early Years Settings*. Wolverhampton: Early Years Equality

Lane, J (1996) *From Cradle to School*. London: Commission for Racial Equality.

Lane, J (2008) *Young Children and Social Justice: understanding the past, thinking about the present, planning for the future*. London: National Children's Bureau.

Longfield, A (2007) 'In my view: Why let children take part?' in *Nursery World* 28 June.

McClement, E 'Persona Dolls in Action: an exploration of the use of the Dolls as an antidiscriminatory intervention in the classroom'. Unpublished dissertation.

MacNaughton, G (1993) 'A poststructuralist analysis of learning in early childhood settings'. Paper presented to the Pre-Conference Symposium at the 2nd annual conference of Australian Research in Early Childhood Education, Canberra.

MacNaughton, G (1995) 'Girls, Boys and Race: where's the power?' Conference paper, Washington National Association for the Education of Young Children, December.

MacNaughton, G (1996) The Gender Factor in B. Creasner and E. Dau (eds) *The Anti-Bias Approach in Early Childhood*. Sydney: HarperEducational.

MacNaughton, G (1999) 'Dolls for Equity: Young Children Learning Respect and Un-learning unfairness'. Paper presented to the Persona Doll Conference, London.

MacNaughton, G (1999) Even pink tents have glass ceilings: crossing the gender boundaries in pretend play, in E Dau and E Jones (eds), *Child's Play: Revising Play in Early Childhood Settings*. Sydney: MacLennan and Petty.

MacNaughton, G (2000) *Rethinking Gender in Early Childhood Studies*. London: Routledge/Falmer.

MacNaughton, G (2005) *Doing Foucault in Early Childhood Education*. London: Paul Chapman.

MacNaughton, G (2007) 'Equity and Respect for Diversity: critical meaning making a key competency for professionals'. Paper presented to the conference, 'That's not fair', Kinderwelten project, Berlin, Germany.

MacNaughton, G and Williams G (1998) *Techniques for Teaching Young Children: choices in theory and practice*. Australia: Addison Wesley Longman.

Macpherson, W *et al* (1999) *The Stephen Lawrence Inquiry*. London: The Stationery Office.

Mathias, B and French, M (1996) *40 Ways To Raise a Nonracist Child*. New York: HarperCollins.

McKee, D (1989) *Elmer the Patchwork Elephant*. Glasgow: HarperCollins.

Miles, B (2006) 'Teaching about the abolition of the Atlantic slave trade: principles to adopt, pitfalls to avoid' in *Race Equality Teaching* 25 (1).

Milner, D (1983) *Children and Race: Ten Years On*. London: Ward Lock Educational.

Muslim Council of Britain (2007) *Meeting the Needs of Muslim Pupils in State Schools: Information and Advice for Schools*. Muslim Council of Britain.

Naidoo, B (first published 1985. Current edn. 2008) *Journey to Jo'burg*. Glasgow: HarperCollins.

Newstead, S (2006) *The Buskers Guide to Anti-discriminatory education*. Hampshire: Common Threads.

Norwich, B 'Special Needs Education or Education for All? Connective specialisation and ideological impurity' in *British Journal of Special Education* 3.

O'Connor, A. (2008) 'Pretty in pink' in *London Nursery World* 3 January.

Ofsted (1999) *Raising the attainment of minority ethnic pupils – school and LEA responses*. London: Ofsted.

Ofsted (2003) *The education of asylum-seeker pupils*. London: Ofsted.

Paley, V (1995) *Kwanza and me: a teacher's story*. Cambridge: Harvard University Press.

Penn, H (2000) 'Hopes and Fears' in *Nursery World* 13 January.

Qualifications and Curriculum Authority (2000) *Curriculum Guidance for the Foundation Stage*. London: Qualifications and Curriculum Authority.

Richardson, R (2007) 'Getting them together: the equalities agenda in education, autumn 2007 and beyond' in *Race Equality Teaching*, 26 (1).

Richman, N (1998) *In the Midst of the Whirlwind*. Stoke-on-Trent: Trentham Books.

Rieser, R and Mason, M (1990) *Disability Equality in the Classroom: a human rights issue*. London: Equality in Education.

Rutter, J (1994) *Refugee Children in the Classroom*. Stoke-on-Trent: Trentham Books.

Saunders, K *Happy Ever Afters: a storybook guide to teaching children about disability*. Stoke-on-Trent: Trentham Books.

Schiller, C (1974) cited by S Maxwell in *Preparation for Teaching in Reflections on Early Education and Care Inspired by Visits to Reggio Emilia, Italy*. London: British Association for Early Childhood Education.

Scott, B (2008) *Glasgow Antiracist Curriculum: an approach for early years centres*. Glasgow: Glasgow City Council

Selleck, D and Griffin, S (1996) Quality for the Under-Threes, in G. Pugh (ed) *Contemporary issues in the Early Years: Working Collaboratively for Children*. London: Paul Chapman.

Sheppy, S (2008) *Personal, Social and Emotional Development in the EYFS*. London: David Fulton.

Silin, J (1995) *Sex, Death and the Education of Children: Our Passion for Ignorance in the Age of AIDS*. New York: Teachers College Press.

Silin, J (1999) 'Speaking up for silence' in *Australian Journal of Early Childhood* 24 (4).

Silin, J (2002) 'Talking with children about difficult issues' in *Centre for Equity and Innovation in Early Childhood CEIEC Members' issues* paper 1.

Silin, J (2005) Silence, Voice and Pedagogy, in N. Yelland (ed.) *Critical Issues in Early Childhood Education*. Berkshire, Open University Press.

Smidt, S (1998) *A guide to early years practice*. Routledge: London.

Smidt, S (2007) *Supporting Multilingual Learners in the Early Years*. London: Routledge.

Siraj-Blatchford, I (1994) *The early years: laying the foundations for racial equality*. Stoke-on-Trent: Trentham Books.

Siraj-Blatchford, I (1995) Racial Equality Education: identity, curriculum and pedagogy, in J Siraj-Blatchford and I Siraj-Blatchford (eds) *Educating the Whole Child*. Buckingham: Open University Press.

Siraj-Blatchford, I and Clarke, P (2000) *Supporting identity, diversity and language in the early years*. Buckingham: Open University Press.

Sutcliffe, S and Sutcliffe, B (1995) *Committed to Sikhism*. Norwich: RMEP.

Taus, K (1987) 'Teachers as storytellers for justice'. Unpublished master's thesis, Pacific Oaks College, Pasadena, C.A.

Troyna, B and Hatcher, R (1992) *Racism in Children's Lives: a study of mainly white primary schools*. London: Routledge.

United Nations Convention on the Rights of the Child (1990).

Whitney, T (1999) *Kids Like Us: Using Persona Dolls*. St Paul: Redleaf.

Wood, D and Wood, H (1983) 'Questioning the Pre-school Child' in *Educational Review* 35 (2).

Wood, E and Atfield, J (1996) *Play Learning and the Early Childhood Curriculum*. London: Paul Chapman.

Wright, C (1992) *Race relations in the primary school*. London: David Fulton.

Index